Building Bridges and Viaducts
FOR MODEL RAILWAYS

Building Bridges and Viaducts
FOR MODEL RAILWAYS

Bob Alderman

THE CROWOOD PRESS

First published in 2014 by
The Crowood Press Ltd
Ramsbury, Marlborough
Wiltshire SN8 2HR

www.crowood.com

British Library Cataloguing-in-Publication Data
A catalogue record for this book is available from the British Library.

ISBN 978 1 84797 818 9

Disclaimer
The author and the publisher do not accept any responsibility in any manner
whatsoever for any error or omission, or any loss, damage, injury, adverse outcome,
or liability of any kind incurred as a result of the use of any of the information
contained in this book, or reliance upon it.

Acknowledgements
I have had help from many friends and others in the preparation of this book. In
particular to Graham Tombs for his help in going back to his day job to give me
practical guidance on various structures; Dave Sapp for his holiday diversion for the
Welsh Highland Railway pictures; and Geoff Byman for his input on the garden railway
structures. Others too who have kindly supplied photographs where I have been
unable to access some bridges. Finally to those who presented me with their work at
model railway exhibitions that I was able to photograph.

Typeset by Jean Cussons Typesetting, Diss, Norfolk
Printed and bound in India by Replika Press Pvt Ltd

CONTENTS

INTRODUCTION

Bridges and viaducts have been a necessity for railway engineers from the beginning of railways. Natural features like valleys and rivers have to be crossed; man-made features like roads and canals have to be crossed too. Sometimes the construction of the railway required bridges for roads above railway cuttings or below embankments.

The world's first railway bridge was the Causey Arch near Stanley, County Durham – a masonry arch built in 1725–26 to carry a plateway over the Bobgins' Burn. The preserved line of the Tanfield Railway is nearby and Beamish Open Air Museum is close. The first railway viaduct was in Blaenafon, South Wales though its remains have been lost.

The earliest railway engineers worked in stone, wood and cast and wrought iron; steel came later to railway structures. Many of these steel structures are still present and in use.

Wood generally has not had the same longevity. Brunel used it extensively in viaducts to cross Cornish valleys. All his viaducts have been replaced in masonry and brick, leaving only the plinths that supported the timber trusses. However, a fine later timber structure still exists in use across the estuary of the Afon Mawddach, Barmouth, Gwynedd.

Early cast-iron structures have not lasted either. Often they failed, as the material was not used to its best advantage. One early structure is the Gaunless Bridge constructed by Robert Stephenson, once part of the Stockton and Darlington Railway at West Auckland, which has now been re-erected outside the National Railway Museum, York. Later ones remain in use and are generally of monumental proportions. Some part cast-iron bridges remain: the ironwork left from an earlier period used as decoration and a newer internal structure used for load-carrying.

Steel is widely used and can be seen everywhere. It is commonly used in the simple plate-girder bridge.

Here steel sections and plates are riveted together to form a larger girder or sections joined to make up truss-girder bridges. A modern application is the welding of plate to form box girder bridges.

Widely used in the present is reinforced concrete; these structures often show great simplicity of form.

BRIDGE TYPES

MASONRY AND BRICK

There is regional variation following house styles for many of the masonry and brick structures, though they all have the same basic construction. In addition, the local geology has much to do with the variation. The local stone will have a characteristic colour and texture. Similarly the clays available for brick-making each imparted different colours. In the case of bricks, some national uniformity crept in once mass production was undertaken and especially with the production of the hard engineering bricks, Staffordshire Blue being very common.

STEEL

Steel structures are generally consistent throughout the country. This is down to the engineering principles that are used to fabricate a structure to span a gap. Plate-girder bridges are probably the most common. Truss-girder bridges are less so and have more specific applications. The Dapol Girder Bridge is an over-simplified version of one of these.

IRON

Iron bridges are immediately recognizable from their monumental appearance. The usual form is a segmental arch and is often highly decorated, exploiting this feature of cast iron.

CONCRETE

Again modern concrete construction shows great

consistency across the country. The sizes range from small occupation crossings to bridges carrying multiple tracks across major roads.

MODELS

I have set out to give examples of many of these structures, which are by no means all-inclusive. They are illustrated and described in the following chapters. I believe that if there is some understanding of how something is made, a better model will result. I have made several of these structures with step-by-step illustrations. They have been constructed in plasticard sheet, embossed and plain, and plastic sections. This is my preferred medium for structures – it can be readily cut, joined and shaped.

All but one of the models has been made in 7mm: 1ft scale. Partly because this is the scale I usually work in, but it also makes the models large enough to illustrate the construction. The methods I have used should read across to the smaller scales too.

The models have been made and photographed as the build progressed. This has resulted in odd corners of my workshop turning up in the background. I trust this will not be too distracting!

Other models are illustrated from commercial sources and some that other modellers have made.

CHAPTER ONE

PROTOTYPE DESCRIPTIONS

MASONRY ARCH BRIDGES AND VIADUCTS

Arch bridges and viaducts fall into three main types: semi-circular or Roman arch, segmental (a segmental arch is part of a circle) or elliptical. Elliptical arches seem to be rare in viaducts, though, simple curves being preferred. All types can be found around the system.

The main parts of a masonry arch are:

- Abutments that support the ends of the arch providing the base for the arch or, for a viaduct, a column or pier.
- The arch on the abutments.
- Spandrels filling the space above the arch.
- The parapet above the spandrel. This is often separated from the spandrel by a string course of stone or brick standing proud of the face.

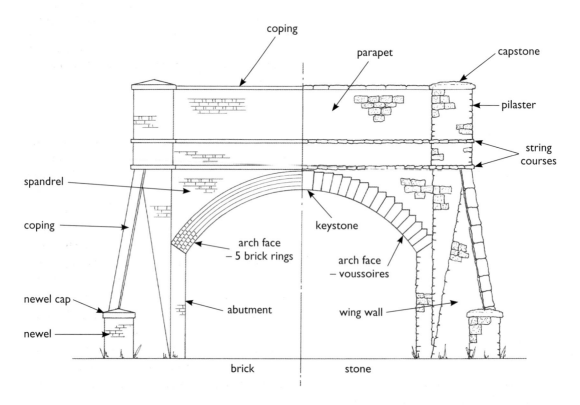

The principal parts of a bridge. Illustrated is a segmental arch; a semi-circular arch would be of the same construction. The drawing has been divided on the centreline to show both brick and stone construction. Most features are common, except when turning the arch. In brick, several rings of brick are laid continuously around the arch. In stone there are a series of blocks – the voussoire style is shown here, though they can be a series of radially jointed blocks. In either case there will be a keystone at the top of the arch. A brick arch may also be finished with either style of stone arch end.

- The wing walls to the sides of each abutment, if the bridge is on an embankment. Note that the wing wall leans back into the embankment face; this is called batter. The slope is generally around 1 in 8.

To construct a bridge, first the abutments and wing walls are built. When a railway was being constructed these would initially stand alone, either alongside the river or road, and the embankment would be constructed butting up to them. In the case of a viaduct, there is no abutment at each end, only an end pier.

A detail of a brick arch. There are four rows of bricks forming this arch; there can be a lot more. The abutments to the ends will have been built first, the wooden centring would have been fitted and the arch bricks laid on this. Once complete the spandrels would follow to the top of the parapet. Note how the bricks fit on to the abutment.

These abutments were built for a bridge on a railway that was never constructed: The Portmadoc, Beddgelert & South Snowdon Railway. The support for the bridge sits as a large pillar, the roadway face vertical and the embankment side is stepped, reducing in thickness towards the top. The mass is needed at the bottom for stability. The wing wall is tied into either side, which gives the opportunity to see what is hidden on other bridges. It is an unusual survivor from c.1901 and can be found in a field near Beddgelert. DAVID SAPP

The arches are constructed by erecting a wooden structure, called centring, which will rest on the abutment or pier, or even on the ground. This makes a surface upon which the brick or stone of the arch is built. It is a temporary support until the arch supports itself. For more than one span there may be two or three or more sets of centring, each moving on to make the next arch as an arch is completed.

With the arch in place, the spandrels are constructed up to the level of the base of the trackwork or roadway. The space between the spandrels and the arch is then filled with rubble to provide a continuous surface across the top of the arch. The sides are completed by a parapet. The embankment is then completed up to the abutment and wing walls.

ARCH CONSTRUCTION

A brick arch usually consists of several rings of brick laid with the longest part of the brick along the axis of the arch. The bricks are usually laid with stretcher bond. With a brick arch there is no keystone unless

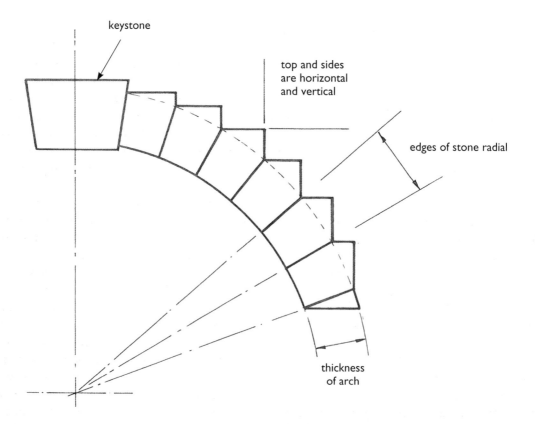

keystone

top and sides are horizontal and vertical

edges of stone radial

thickness of arch

ABOVE: **This shows the geometry of voussoirs. The inner edge of the stones follow the curve of the arch and outer ends are finished to have vertical and horizontal edges defined by the thickness of the arch.**

ABOVE AND RIGHT: **A stone arch with similar width stones on the face and quoin finish to the inside of the arch. The keystone on the face can just be made out behind the height restriction sign.**

the face of the bridge is finished in stone with a stone arch on the end.

A stone arch is generally similar except for the larger size of the stones in the arch. Again, the longest part of the stone is along the axis of the arch. The appearance of a stone arch can vary at the end of the arch. The stones can be shaped as even blocks with radial joints and completed with a keystone at the top of the arch. These stones are laid as quoins, alternating long and short into the arch. These shapes are most obvious on the external corners of structures. Alternatively they can be finished with a form known as 'voussoirs'. These are shaped with an end conforming to the shape of the arch and the end where the spandrel sits is finished with horizontal and vertical surfaces. Again, the part of the voussoirs inside the arch alternate between long and short, the same as a quoin.

Complications arise with both stone and brick arches when the axis of the arch is not square to the axis of the route above. The bricks or stones are laid as 'winding courses'; that is they appear to spiral around the arch. Simplistically, to get this correct, the brick or stone joints notionally along the arch axis have to end square to the end of the arch. The mathematics of the construction is complex.

Stone voussoirs on a skewed arch. The internal winding brickwork of the arch can be seen sloping parallel to the internal joints between the voissoirs. Consider the work of the masons cutting these stones.

STEEL BRIDGES

For simple steel bridges there are either plate girders or trusses. The choice of one over the other is usually determined by cost for a relative span. Plate girders are preferred for spans between 30 and 80ft (9–24m), though there are longer ones. A lattice truss is preferred for spans of 150 to 220ft (46–67m). Greater spans can be achieved by adding supports at appropriate distances.

Steel bridges of either form are *never* curved in planform. If the track is on a curve, then the bridge will be series of straight units following the curve like the edge of a 50p coin, a polygon.

For a single track, a girder or truss is sufficient each side. The loads will twist the structure and lead to rapid failure. If there is more than one track, then substantial cross-girders are required to support further longitudinal girders below each rail. On double tracks there will be three plate girders: one each outside and a third between the tracks. The plate girder between the tracks has to be twice the strength of an outer girder. The overall dimensions may be the same but the web material thicknesses will be twice that of the outer. Often the centre girder will have a reduced height with consequent further increases in material thicknesses. For modelling purposes this can be ignored!

PLATE GIRDER

The main parts of steel bridge are:

- The main girders that span the gap, which can be fabricated from plates and sections, either riveted or welded together. The forms the girder can take are either an 'I' section or, for a modern welded structure, a box.
- Separating the main girders from side to side there are girders that provide the support to the trackbed or roadway. The track support can be a longitudinal girder supporting timber baulks that the track is fixed to, or a ballast layer is present as the track support.
- The abutments support the main girders in masonry, brick or concrete. The abutments

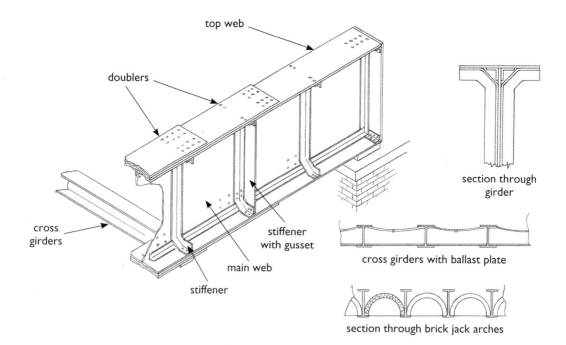

top web

doublers

cross girders

stiffener with gusset

main web

stiffener

section through girder

cross girders with ballast plate

section through brick jack arches

The principal parts of a plate girder. The section of a plate girder is an 'I'. The vertical part is a web and the top and bottom are closed off with smaller webs. These webs are progressively doubled in thickness on longer spans to increase the resistance to bending. The doublers on the webs may not be symmetrical. The top web has to resist compressive forces and the bottom tension forces. The main web is divided by stiffeners, which are spaced either to make square panels in the vertical web or a little further apart, about 1.3 x the height of the vertical web. Some stiffeners may have an additional gusset to further stiffen them. The ends of the stiffeners are forged around the corner to miss the angles that join the webs. As drawn they are distinctly angular in the corner, but on some bridges they may be more curved. See the section through the girder. The whole is assembled with rivets, though more modern bridges are welded.

The floor of the bridge can be completed with plates that the ballast sits on. These plates are usually dished and have a drain at the lowest point. Small brick jack arches sitting on the cross girders are common: the gaps above are filled with small stones and the ballast bed is laid on them. The cross girder may have longitudinal girders with longitudinal timber baulks to carry the track: this construction may be open or be closed off with platework with ballast on top.

A plate-girder bridge on the West Somerset Railway. The load-carrying structure is painted black. The Great Western 'stone' colour is a steel parapet. Bridges of the style where the girders are inside the pilaster are not popular with bridge inspectors, as it is difficult to assess their condition at the ends.

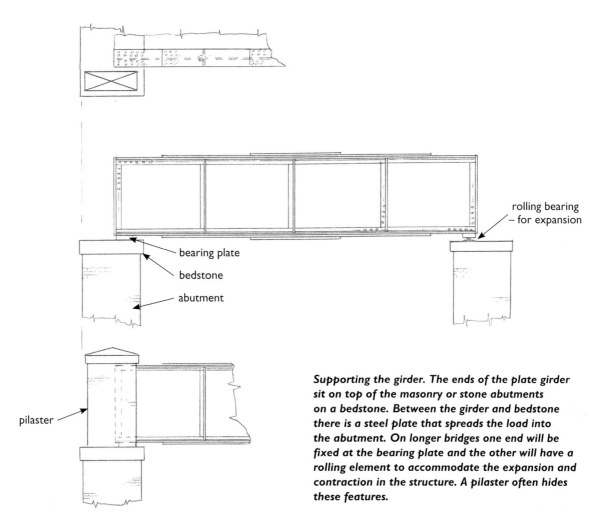

rolling bearing – for expansion

bearing plate

bedstone

abutment

pilaster

Supporting the girder. The ends of the plate girder sit on top of the masonry or stone abutments on a bedstone. Between the girder and bedstone there is a steel plate that spreads the load into the abutment. On longer bridges one end will be fixed at the bearing plate and the other will have a rolling element to accommodate the expansion and contraction in the structure. A pilaster often hides these features.

will have pads and a location for the girder to be located on. There is provision for the bridge assembly to move as it expands and contracts with temperature differences. One end of the bridge will rest on bearing pads; the other will have provision for the movement due to expansion, for example rollers.
- The wing walls to the sides of each abutment, if the bridge is on an embankment.
- There are differences in the way the supporting girders are filled between each girder. Small brick arches can be constructed in each gap – these are called jack arches. An alternative is for plate work to be fitted between each girder – these plates belly downwards and at the lowest point often have a drain.

- Alongside the girder there will be plates to retain the ballast and prevent it being in direct contact with the main girder, as an anti-corrosion measure.

The construction of a girder bridge requires the abutment and wing walls to be built first. The main girders are then craned into place to rest on the abutments and the cross-girder structure completed once they are in place.

TRUSS GIRDER

A truss-girder bridge is made up of assemblies of steel section, usually riveted together to form lattice girders and struts. These present a much more open construction than other bridges – the triangle fea-

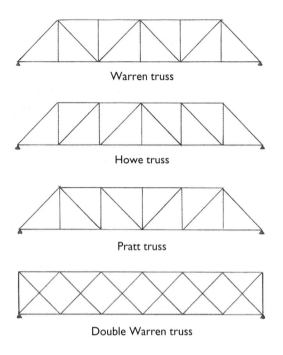

Warren truss

Howe truss

Pratt truss

Double Warren truss

Truss types. Illustrated are the basic outlines of the four main truss types used. The Warren truss is common in Britain. The girderwork in the truss can range from simple 'I' and 'H' sections riveted or bolted together with gusset plates at the joints to more complex fabricated girders with their own diagonal bracing.

tures largely; in some respects they replicate earlier wooden structures. The photographs show the complexity of the girders.

There are several basic types of truss, which vary according to the geometry of the members. They are installed as either a through truss, where the girders are above the deck, or a deck truss, where the girders are below the deck. The former are favoured in the UK, whilst the latter are used around the world and are common in the USA.

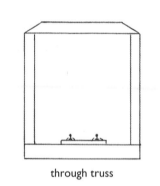

through truss

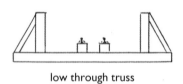

low through truss

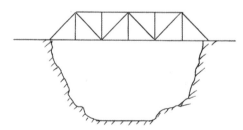

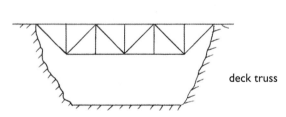

deck truss

Trusses can be used with girderwork configured to be above the track or below it. Above it is a 'through truss' and below a 'deck truss'. The through truss is common in Britain. Note that in both cases the trusses are stabilized with girders crossing left to right. An exception is a low through truss where the deck girders are extended beyond the truss and a diagonal brace added.

Cogload Junction truss-girder bridge. This bridge is situated 5 miles (8km) east of Taunton station where the line diverges to Castle Cary. It allows the line from Bristol to fly over the line coming in from Castle Cary. The girders in this structure are fabricated, leading to an intricate structure with crossed members forming the webs with many rivets.

The installation of a truss-girder bridge follows that of a plate girder bridge having the same features.

A feature of a truss girder is its response to the applied load. To prevent distortion, the top or bottom girders are tied together by spanning girders: top girders for the through truss; bottom for a deck truss. For a lower height truss, the deck-supporting beams are extended beyond the sides and braces erected from them to the top girder.

IRON BRIDGES

A surprising number of cast-iron bridges remain; they are generally large structures. One of the features of the material is that it allows considerable decoration to be added to the casting, of which the engineers of the time took full advantage. The style

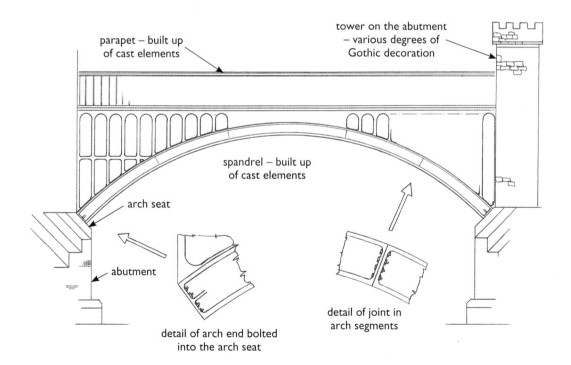

Iron bridge features. Iron bridges often use embellishments that cast iron allows; often Gothic forms. The basic bridge is series of arch segments bolted together and sections of cast spandrel elements bolted to these. The arch is seated on the abutment so that the loading is squarely directed into the structure. The parapet is a series of cast elements bolted together, often carrying the most embellishment. The masonry structures continue the Gothic embellishment.

One of several iron bridges in and around Castlefield, Manchester. This one is across the Rochdale Canal above the bottom lock. Cast iron has been used to create elaborate detail above the arch.

of the decoration often follows neo-Gothic, as that was hugely popular during the time these bridges were constructed (c.1850–80).

A bridge will consist of a number of segmental arches laid side by side and joined by a secondary spacing structure and a deck on top. The inner arches do not usually carry any decoration. Each arch is built up from a number of segments bolted together. The joints between the segments on the inner arches are generally more visible than those on the outside arches. Rather than a parapet, the top is completed with cast-iron decorative railings. The buttresses are in substantial stonework, again with Gothic details such as castellated turrets.

CONCRETE

This material is favoured for modern bridges. The concrete is either reinforced with an internal mesh of steel bars – reinforced concrete – or has tensioned bars within the concrete beam – pre-stressed concrete. Unless there is a failure of the concrete, the internal components are invisible. There may be some evidence of pre-stressed structure by small filled patches along a beam.

A concrete structure is generally quite plain, though sometimes a decorative finish may be applied.

The bridge deck may be a series of rectangular beams placed side by side on to the abutment or a series of interlocking shaped beams. Abutments may be the original from an earlier girder bridge with modified bedplate for the beams to rest on. For new

A concrete bridge on the Yeovil–Dorchester line to the north of Dorchester, crossing the Dorchester ring road. It barely shows but the parapet has a random stone finish cast in. There is a similar one at the Weymouth side of the ring road.

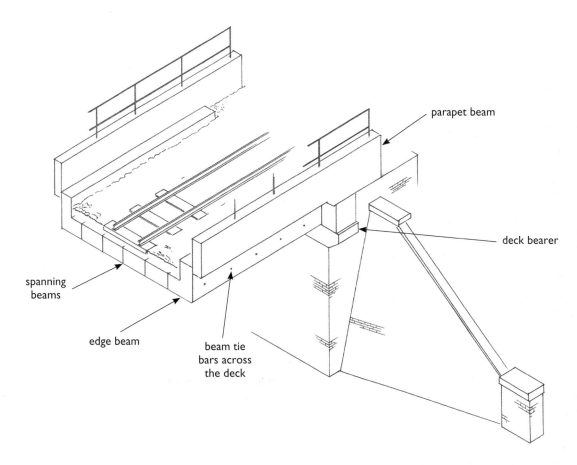

spanning beams

edge beam

beam tie bars across the deck

parapet beam

deck bearer

This is the simplest of the concrete bridge structures. A series of beams spans the gap between the abutments. The edges are completed with beams that have provision to retain the ballast; this may also extend to carry the safety rails on the parapet or a secondary beam may be used for this purpose. The beams are pulled together by stressed steel elements fitted across them. The evidence for these can be seen with small regularly spaced patches on the edge of the outside beam. The abutments may be those from an earlier steel girder bridge. In this case they will have been modified to accept a concrete deck bearer. A new bridge abutment will have this incorporated in its basic structure.

or total replacement bridges, the abutment will be wholly cast in situ in reinforced concrete.

Parapets may be a secondary structure providing the lateral retention of ballast and the location for hand-rails.

EARTHWORKS

Earthworks of varying degree accompany every bridge installation – these are the cuttings and embankments. Cuttings are made to keep a level road through rising ground and embankments to fill where the ground falls away. During construction, material from a cutting would often be used to form the next embankment. Often where a road would cross the railway at the same level, the road climbs on to an embankment to cross the railway with a bridge.

An essential feature of cuttings and embankments is that the slopes should be stable: too steep and they will slide down. This can be illustrated by pouring salt on to a surface: it forms a pyramid with

An embankment east of Crewkerne, Somerset. This embankment raises the railway to cross a shallow valley. To the left it is pierced by a highway bridge. The relationship between the embankment and the abutment can be clearly seen, in contrast to the many places where it is obscured by growth on the slopes.

a set slope to the sides; the slope remains the same no matter how high the pile – it has natural stability. So it is with various soils, gravels and crushed rock. The civil engineer working with these materials sets out to match these slopes. This has to be determined for the location when constructing the line. Whether it is an embankment or cutting, the slope will be the same.

Rock is generally more stable than soil so can hold a steeper or near vertical slope. The strength of a rock is usually referred to as its competency; the ability to hold its slope, zero or more degrees. However, alongside the railway a rock face slopes away from the trackbed, avoiding potentially unsafe overhangs. This angle, like the lean on a bridge wing

wall, is called batter. A brick or stone-block sided cutting or embankment can be treated as if it is rock, having similar batter.

Typical slopes for different materials are illustrated.

It is clear on the railways of today that the tops of embankments are no longer wide enough to accommodate the modern track standards. The track now has a substantial ballast shoulder at the ends of the sleepers that requires more width in the formation. To accommodate this, supports are sometimes added along the top of the embankment, especially where it is not possible to nominally increase the width by using more ballast. This is frequently seen beside bridges.

A cutting east of Yeovil Junction Station. Here it is a case of two for the price of one: the lower part of the cutting is in local sandstone and the upper in softer material and soils. The sandstone is sufficiently competent to hold a near vertical surface, whilst the upper is a nominal slope of 45 degrees – if it can be made out from the overgrown state.

Board supports for the ballast shoulder. The boards themselves are held by what appear to be scaffolding tubes driven into the formation. The parapet railing has been extended over the boarded area as the notional bridge deck has been extended.

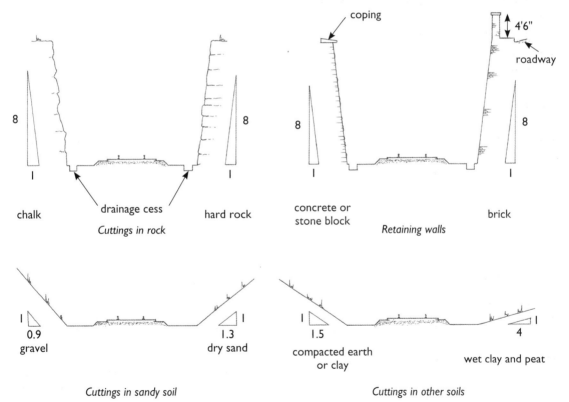

chalk   drainage cess   hard rock

Cuttings in rock

coping

4'6"

roadway

concrete or stone block   brick

Retaining walls

0.9 gravel   1.3 dry sand

Cuttings in sandy soil

1.5 compacted earth or clay   4 wet clay and peat

Cuttings in other soils

Earthworks on the railway vary in geometry depending on the soil or rock types. Rocks are described as 'competent' by their ability to withstand crushing. The better they are at this, the nearer vertical the rock face can be. In general, vertical rock faces are not used and have a batter of 1 in 8. The same applies to concrete, stone or brick, being manmade 'rock faces'. Soil types have different competency or ability to hold a slope: this is known as the angle of repose. No matter how high they are piled, the slope will always be the same. The illustration shows cuttings but the reverse holds for embankments.

CHAPTER TWO

ILLUSTRATIONS OF BRIDGES AND VIADUCTS

In no particular order, illustrations are presented here of bridges and viaducts from around the country. Some are in current use, others are on closed lines. There is a surprisingly large number of structures still standing that are no longer in railway use.

Note that all the pictures have been taken from public access points of view – there has been no trespass on railway property. Be warned that such trespass can be lethal.

BRICK-ARCH BRIDGES

The photographs illustrate a number of different types of masonry bridges, in brick and stone. The arch forms are all present. Different details are picked out and described.

A blue brick segmental arch bridge. Note the modern addition of the yellow and black warning stripes to define the arch and the definition of the maximum height envelope in white paint on the parapet. This example is at Keinton Mandeville in Somerset.

A detail showing the wing wall, abutments, pilaster and parapet. Note the striped appearance of the brickwork. This is shown more clearly in the illustration of the detailed brickwork. Note also the weathering of the string course stones – the one under the warning triangle has lost an edge.

A detail of the brickwork; it is English bond. The bricks are laid alternating between stretchers, laid long ways, and headers, laid with the length into the wall. These are engineering blue bricks. The differences in colours are down to temperature differences during the firing: the full blue has achieved the highest temperature, whilst the red-shaded areas have achieved a slightly lower temperature. This effect results in the stripes.

At first glance this appears to be a Gothic arch but it is a series of narrow arches side by side but displaced one to another. This bridge is a substantial structure carrying a further earth embankment carrying two tracks above the arches. The result of this creates a long arch, which may have made difficulties if it were a skew arch. Note that there are two sets of safety rails: one above the arch and the other higher beside the track.

A nearer view of the multiple arches: there are six in all. It can be seen they quite narrow: about 12ft (3.6m) wide, but the width of the bridge along the road is around 60ft (18m). There are a number of tie rods showing on the spandrel and there are further ones on the inner arches too.

This is long, low arch again piercing an embankment with further earthworks on top. This is constructed as a skew arch. The road is unclassified – a lane. It occupies the centre of the arch for maximum height, whilst on both sides of the lane there is small watercourse.

A small semi-circular arch occupation bridge on the Severn Valley Railway at Kidderminster. The wing walls here are asymmetric, the left-hand one being nominally square to the spandrel but the right-hand one is at an angle to allow for the turn of the roadway. In consequence it becomes longer. The wing walls are capped with profiled bricks rather than stones. There is no string course so the parapet rises out of the spandrels. Note the modern security fencing at the top of the embankment.

A red brick arch, one of a pair side by side at Maiden Newton on the line between Yeovil and Weymouth. The second slightly different shaped arch can be made out beyond the near one. It appears to be a damp situation by the growth and staining on the brickwork. The parapet is a boarded fence alongside the platform that runs across the bridge.

STONE-ARCH BRIDGES

A skewed arch bridge just west of Yeovil Junction on the Waterloo–Exeter line. The stone, inferior oolite, is very likely to have come from the cutting that Yeovil Junction station sits in. In spite of this the arch is still turned in brick. The arch is of note too, as it is neither semi-circular nor elliptical but a cross between the two. Note the wing wall that starts parallel to the spandrel wall and then curves around to hold back the embankment. It is somewhat lost in the undergrowth though. It seems to be a common feature of the railways today that the cuttings, embankments and structures are not as clear of large growth as they were at one time.

The winding courses of brickwork of the bridge inside the arch. Note the stone wedges that allow the bricks to meet the abutment squarely.

Further west along the Waterloo–Exeter line at Crewkerne, a road-bridge sits on the platform. This has an elliptical arch. Note on each platform the brick pillars, and above each a plain patch in the stonework. This is evidence of an earlier footbridge. Even now the arch seems to show signs of smoke staining from the passage of steam trains.

The bridge at Bishops Lydeard Station on the West Somerset Railway. This a segmental arch turned in brick. Unlike the other arches illustrated, this one uses the bricks as if they have been laid in a wall alternating long and short rather than the simple layering in others. As this is a preserved railway, the bridge still collects smoke stains – a feature now largely lost on the main network.

Another bridge built for the railway that was never constructed; The Portmadoc, Beddgelert & South Snowdon Railway; now in use as means of crossing the road. It can be found just south of the Royal Goat Hotel, Beddgelert. Note the parapet and wing walls are topped with alternating heights of stones known as 'cock and hen'. DAVID SAPP

The road bridge at Ais Gill crossing the Settle and Carlisle line. It is made in the local limestone but the string course and capping stones are made of Penrith Sandstone with its distinctive ginger colour. Note the cutting it spans has shallow slopes to its sides requiring the additional smaller arches for the span. A similar situation can occur for a wider and/or deeper cutting.

An occupation crossing on the Settle and Carlisle line. The wing walls unusually splay towards the opening rather than away from it.

Two occupation crossings on the closed line to Garsdale Junction on the Settle and Carlisle line at Hawes. The embankments on each crossing slope sideways towards a reduced wing wall as well as the main slope from the trackbed to the field. Curiously, one has a field boundary wall running through the arch.

This bridge illustrates the influence of the major local landowner wanting to look at something out of the ordinary. It is at Grimstone north of Dorchester on the Yeovil–Weymouth line. The spandrels are pierced with secondary arches and the main arch abutment is also pierced with arches. The left-hand arch has a small stream running through it and the right-hand one is a relic of the Second World War, a concrete 'dragons tooth' anti-tank measure that once, with others, blocked the main arch.

An elliptical arch at Yeovil Pen Mill Station. This bridge is entirely constructed in local stone, Inferior Oolite, including the arch. Note the voissoirs around the arch and the prominent keystone.

PLATE-GIRDER BRIDGES

The bridges illustrated range from simple girders to more substantial ones. Often the simple ones are for secondary roads crossing the railway, whilst the substantial ones carry the railway across significant spans. Again details noted.

BELOW: *A road over a bridge at Chetnole Halt on the Yeovil to Weymouth line. The bridge consists of four girders spanning the railway, which rest on abutments that are a mixture of stone and blue brick. Between each girder are brick jack arches that support the roadway. On the right-hand abutment there is a limited clearance warning plate. The other side of the line clearly has more room. The parapet is secondary to the girders. Note the gap between the plate and the pilaster.*

The bridge plate superseding earlier stencilled information. The 'WEY' refers to Weymouth district; the number's origins are lost but probably follow on from the original numbering system from when the line was built. The distance, remaining firmly in imperial units from historical records, is the distance from Paddington.

A detail of the jack arches. Blue bricks are laid in stretcher bond across the span. The doublers seem to be a repair as they are bolted not riveted and just to one side of the bridge, and include a tie-bar between them.

The parapet of the Chetnole bridge. There is a kerb across the whole span preventing water ingress to the girder below and the capping stones of the pilasters are flush with the brickwork on the road side but have an overlap on the railway side. The plate on the nearest pilaster identifies the bridge.

A detail of the mid-span support of the bridge shown below. The end webs of each plate girder are riveted together, making the joint between the two. The girders are resting on blue brick pier capped with concrete. The safety rails at this point are supported with two different styles of stanchions: to the left, angle iron curved around with a small bracing web, and to the right similar but with a larger bracing web. Both are attached to the top web of the girder.

A pair of plate-girder bridges in a succession of bridges and viaducts across the flood plain of the River Parrett near Langport, Somerset. This particular span is over a flood defence embankment. Note the corrosion breaking through the paint.

A girder bridge on the skew. Note the various warning chevrons: the ones on the girder have been applied as separate plates; the one on the abutment is the standard one used by highways indicating a restricted clearance. The parapet here is made from a lattice of strips riveted together and to a T-section top and bottom.

A close-up of the previous bridge showing the U-shaped channel decking. Note the central girder. The supports to the parapet can be more clearly made out. Every other girder web support has been widened at the top to provide a location for the vertical members of the parapet lattice.

ABOVE: *This bridge once carried the North Staffordshire line at Wheelock, Cheshire, across the Trent and Mersey Canal. It is now a farmer's occupation crossing. Note the general lack of paint.*

This small bridge to the west of Yeovil Junction at Stoford once carried two tracks; now only the further half carries the railway.

This is a detail of the ballast plate on the previous bridge. Originally this bridge would have been ballasted across the span and loads taken through the ballast to the cross-girders. Note the drains and the gap at the end. Above, the gap would have had a kerb to prevent the ballast falling through.

Another bridge over a canal, this one carrying the Sheffield–Manchester line over the Peak Forest Canal at the foot of the Marple flight of locks. This had recently been refurbished when photographed. Besides crossing the canal, there is a small road to the left. The bridge carries a height warning sign above the road.

A detail of the structure underneath. The bridge carries double track; each rail of that track will be above one of the deep girders. The girders are tied together by a series of smaller girders and cross-bracing.

A detail of the decks of the Stoford bridge: the railway is on the nearer deck, the other redundant part is now boarded over.

Two bridges carrying the Yeovil–Weymouth line over the A37 at Stratton, north of Dorchester. The road originally passed under the left-hand bridge and the River Wrackle under the right-hand one. Road improvements diverted the northbound carriageway through the river span and culverted the river through the embankment.

A small bridge over a stream on the old Highland line at Fort Augustus (at the south-west end of Loch Ness). The track was laid on longitudinal baulks that sat in the two troughs that remain. These formed the primary load-carrying units of the bridge. The girders that carry the guard-rails are secondary. The gaps between would once have been timbered. JOHN HOBDEN

An example of a bridge where the decking structure has been encased in concrete. The surface of the concrete underneath reflects the wood grain of the shuttering put in place to hold the concrete whilst it was being poured. This could be considered a short-cut when modelling a similar bridge, avoiding the construction of the deck girders.

ABOVE AND OPPOSITE: **This is a departure from the United Kingdom but it serves to illustrate a bridge type in use today, whilst the UK examples have largely disappeared. It is about 20 miles (32km) north of Wellington at Silverstream in Upper Hutt, North Island, New Zealand. It is a series of plate girders resting on concrete piers. Two pairs of girders support the track and are tied together with a series of spacers with diagonal frames. Note the close spacing of the sleepers, only a nominal gap between them. On the top of the sleepers there is a continuous steel strip bolted to each sleeper near the end to maintain the sleeper spacing. There is no pathway for a track maintenance crew alongside either track but refuges have been provided cantilevered from the girders over the sides. Note also the similarity of the joint on a pier to the one illustrated earlier.**

CONCRETE BRIDGES

This rather bland structure was built to carry the Yeovil–Weymouth line over the Dorchester bypass to the south of the town. Like a lot of concrete bridges it embodies no notable features, being entirely functional.

This bridge replaces an earlier girder bridge. The abutments have been remade to accept the pre-stressed concrete beams. A new concrete bearer has been added on top of the brickwork. Tie-bars hold the beams together across the width of the span. Their positions can be made out from the paler marks on the side of beam. The parapet is a secondary beam resting on extensions to the bearer beam.

Another replacement bridge at Bradford on Avon; here the abutments have been only rebuilt to fit a bearer plate for the concrete beams. The parapet is built in Bath Stone and is showing some slight distress. The pipe alongside the parapet, like others, is external to the bridge as the roadway is not deep enough for it to be buried in the carriageway. The lagging suggests it is a water main.

This bridge crosses the Peak Forest Canal at Dukinfield, Greater Manchester, and at first glance this appears to be an iron bridge. It is, however, in concrete and the old outer face of the previous iron bridge has been use to face it. The structure reflects the original iron one, a series of arches side by side. Unusually it carries a plate dating its replacement.

A bridge at Thruxton, near Andover. It carries the branch line to Tidworth Camp over what was once the A303 trunk road. It is a series of pre-stressed concrete beams carried on brick abutments. The tie-bar positions on this structure can be made out by the small rectangular patches on the side of the beam. Note that at some time road improvements have dropped the carriageway to increase clearance under the bridge.

A road bridge carrying the A37 over the Yeovil–Weymouth line beside the southern portal of Evershot Tunnel where, before the road improvements, the road passed over the tunnel. This serves to illustrate the lighter structure of road-bridges compared to railway bridges. Evershot Station before closure sat in this approximate position.

IRON BRIDGES

When I was preparing this book I was surprised at the number of cast-iron structures that still remain and that most of them were still in use. Perhaps it is their monumental nature that has saved them. They were built at a time when embellishment was not a matter of cost but, it seems, a matter of making a statement. This has been recognized on some today by a more elaborate paint scheme than a simple single colour, which makes them very distinctive structures.

Modelling these structures is probably easier if 3D printing and laser cutting of the profiles can be employed.

A detail of the bridge showing the elaborate decoration that can be achieved in cast iron. The connection between the main arch and the deck consists of Gothic arches; the railings above are filigree decorated with fleur-de-lis. The sectional construction of the arch can be made out by the joints between the arches, third from right, and railing sections between the uprights.

The foreground bridge is in cast iron at Castlefield Junction of the Rochdale and Bridgewater canals. It was built in 1849 for the then Manchester, South Junction and Altrincham Railway, later part of the London and North Western Railway, then London Midland and Scottish Railway. It now carries part of the Manchester Metrolink. It is not covered in rust but a rather drab brown paint. Note the brick-built octagonal turrets at each end of the span. The left-hand one has a crenellated top, whilst the right-hand one has lost its top in the passage of time.

A detail of the abutment decoration of the North Road bridge. This is quite elaborate, having twin crenellated turrets and a gargoyle. Note the two remaining telephone insulators on the stonework beside the arch. The early structure is now dominated by the modern pre-cast concrete flyover above.

A detail of the North Road bridge structure; the decorative face with the parapet is held off a second cast-iron set of arches by a series of diagonal girders. A bolted joint can be seen on the inner arch. The arches supporting the roadway are a little more substantial than the outer pairs. These are separated by a series of stays.

The road bridge over the site of North Road Station, Halifax; it remains though the railway has gone. The use of two colours in the paintwork increases the presence of the structure.

A detail of the abutment of the bridge over the Rochdale Canal illustrated earlier. As it is a skew bridge the foot of each arch has to have a separate footing. It repeats the tower and decoration of the bridge at Castlefield Junction. This suggests that the same patterns have been used for both bridges. An unusual feature is the bird box under the second arch – a very secure location.

TRUSS-GIRDER BRIDGES

Truss-girder bridges are used for the longer spans than can be accomplished with a plate girder and for less weight. Originally they were constructed from fabricated steel sections, so involving lots of rivets joining separate components together. Modern versions employ rolled steel sections and are bolted together.

The bridge over the River Parret at Langport, Somerset. It is part of a complex of bridges and viaducts that carry the railway across the flood plain. The plate-girder bridge illustrated earlier can be seen to the right. The truss carries in a single span what these do as a pair. The detailed photos show the complexity of the structure built up from many elements, some forming small trusses in their own right. The main cross-girders underneath are extended to provide support to stabilizing stays at the sides. The deck is supported by these and smaller section longitudinal girders. Note the very lightweight diagonal stays.

The bridge at Cogload Junction east of Taunton, Somerset. This has two asymmetrical trusses, as the line passing beneath is on an acute skew. The buttresses are very deep to accommodate the skew, resulting in the tapering extension to the main truss. The detail picture again shows a complex, built-up structure riveted together. Note that on this bridge, compared to the one at Langport further down the line, the stabilizing girders at the top are within the structure rather than on top. The depth of the structure to achieve the span is greater, so allowing them to be fitted inside the structure with affecting the loading gauge.

Holgate Road bridge carrying the A59 over the East Coast Main Line just south of York Station. This is a version of a Pratt truss, where the diagonal members overlap each other; note too that as they reach to centre of the bridge, they reduce in section. The jack arches supporting the deck are external to the main structure and are now in concrete, replacing the original brick. In the middle of that picture there is a support suspending an overhead electrification cable.

Bryn-y-Felin bridge in the Aberglaslyn Pass near Beddgelert. This is one of the new bridges on the Welsh Highland line. It closely follows the design of the bridge that originally stood here from 1922 until 1999. The original had to be removed as the level of corrosion in the structure had made it unsafe. With rebuilding of the line, its replacement was installed in 2009. DAVID SAPP

Details of the gusseted joints that connect the girders; the fixings are not rivets, as in older structures, but fitted bolts. The holes are slightly smaller than the bolts and the bolt is driven home with a hammer. The bolts are retained with self-locking nuts. Note the H-section girders form channels; on the original bridge these retained water, and with a lack of painting, resulted in the corrosion problems. Here the bridge is on a subtle gradient that will cause the water to run off rather than puddle. A special paint also protects the steelwork. DAVID SAPP

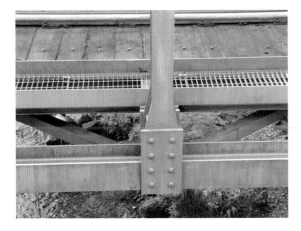

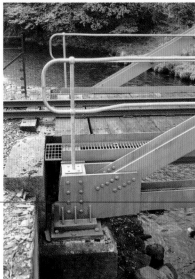

ABOVE AND TOP RIGHT: **Details of the bearing plates sitting on the original abutments: one end of the bridge is secured to the abutment, whilst the other slides on a plate to accommodate expansion and contraction from heating and cooling.** DAVID SAPP

TOP AND BOTTOM LEFT: **Views of the underside of the bridge: the two inner girders are deeper than the others and sit immediately under the rails. The cross-beams extend to make outriggers carrying the mesh walkway. Note the adjacent footbridge made from two arching girders.** DAVID SAPP

A very small truss-girder bridge on the old North Staffs line near the foot of Bosley Locks on the Macclesfield Canal (Ordnance Survey location SJ905657). It spans a small occupation crossing and is also now used as a shed. Between the two pictures the construction can be clearly seen: the Warren truss stabilizes the outer girders, the track sat on the two inner ones.

DAVID KITCHING

VIADUCTS

There are many viaducts around the country – not all in masonry and stone, but also in iron and steel. Some of those illustrated are well-known, others less so. All carry the railway across extended gaps and at various heights.

Ais Gill viaduct, again on the Settle and Carlisle line, is another famed structure at the summit of the line.

Ribblehead Viaduct on the Settle and Carlisle line. It is perhaps one of the most famous of this country's viaducts and is Grade II listed and a Scheduled Ancient Monument. Twenty-four arches carry the line across the River Ribble under Whernside, in North Yorkshire. It is 440 yards long (402m) and at its highest is 104ft (31.7m) above the valley floor. Three of the piers in the span are larger than the others, dividing the structure into four parts.

A detail of one of the arches at Ais Gill. Note the piers each side have been reinforced down their corners with concrete tied to each other with steel rods.

The Cheshire Lines viaducts at Castlefield, Manchester. These Grade II listed structures are essays in wrought and cast iron. The lattice girders are in wrought iron, whilst the columns and decorative work are in cast iron.

A London and North Western Railway viaduct adjacent to Liverpool Road Station, Manchester. It was built c.1867, replacing an earlier structure, and was associated with a warehouse complex. The columns are in cast iron and the girders are wrought iron. Between the girders are semi-circular brick jack arches. Note the intermediate stay rod. The structure is Grade II listed and forms part of the Manchester Museum of Science and Industry (MOSI) complex.

A blue brick viaduct over the River Cary at Somerton, Somerset. The deck of this viaduct has been replaced in concrete for the passage of high-speed trains. The parapet has also been replaced in concrete, though faced with brick to maintain the original appearance. Note the refuges along the parapet – these are gaps with railings. Although appearing to be straight in this view, it follows a gentle curve to the right.

The curvature of the viaduct is exaggerated in the view from a nearby over-bridge. It does serve to show a number of other features too. On the ends of the pilasters there are not only 'Limited Clearance' warning plates, but also 'No Pedestrian Access' signs. The track here is sleepered but the severe foreshortening of the photograph makes it appear otherwise. Over the viaduct each track has guard-rails within the track; should there be a derailment, these are intended to guide the derailed stock over the structure. These rails are the same weight as the running rails and are either attached to the main sleepers or could be attached to sub-sleepers between the main sleepers. The ends are sharply bent around and the ends hidden under a small plate.

Not all viaducts are high. This one is across the flood plain of the River Parrett at Langport in Somerset. The segmental arches are turned in seven rows of bricks and sit on parallel-sided piers. The parapet is low with railings and at every other pier there is refuge that is built out beyond the general envelope of the structure. There is some small decoration: the arches have a ring of half-round brickwork and between the refuges there is a repeat of the corbelled brickwork similar to that at the base of the refuge.

A viaduct just south of Buxton, Derbyshire, on a freight-only line leading to Hindlow Quarry.

A viaduct just north of Chapel-en-le-Frith, Derbyshire. It forms part of a triangle of lines that has two viaducts as part of the triangle; the junction with the second viaduct is just out of sight to the left. Note the massive infill of one of the arches – a little more than the usual jack arch.

TOP: A viaduct in an urban surrounding south of Kidderminster station.

BELOW: Falling Sands Viaduct over the both the River Stour and the Staffs & Worcs Canal at Kidderminster. Note the string course under the parapet is not continuous, stopping abruptly. It appears that the parapet has been rebuilt in part without the decoration. This viaduct carries the Severn Valley Railway.

Cannington Viaduct near Uplyme, Devon, on the closed Lyme Regis branch. It was opened in 1903, four years after Glenfinnan Viaduct on the West Highland Line, which was the first concrete viaduct. This structure is also cast in mass concrete (in solid blocks) with the exception of the sides of the arches, which are cast in individual blocks. The piers rise by steps of 6ft (1.8m), each cast in turn with diminishing size. The tops have corbels that were used to locate the centring for the construction of the arches. During construction one of the piers of the third arch began to settle, cracking the arch. It has been reinforced by two curtain wall jack arches in brick. This structure is Grade II listed.

CHAPTER THREE

BRIDGES AND STRUCTURES: DETAILS

Besides the basic structure of a bridge or viaduct there are other details to look for. There are the refuges where trackworkers can get clear of passing trains. Where required, there are safety rails fitted to the tops of parapets and there are the other items added for improvements or repair.

REFUGES

A parapet of any length will have refuges to permit workers to get clear of passing trains. These can be a masonry balcony above the spandrel wall or a gap in the parapet with guard-rails, or a variation on the two. Sometimes a refuge may be pressed into use to locate additional equipment.

Where there is limited clearance, warning signs are placed at the ends of the structure. If there are refuges, then red and white square warning plates are fitted, which date from around 1950. Where there is very limited clearance and no refuges, then a similar but blue and white plate is fitted, which is a more recent introduction. These are detailed below.

Originally the plate was 12in square but it has now been reduced very slightly to 300mm square.

A width-restriction sign on the end of a parapet extension. In this case there are no refuges on this bridge as it has a short span, and so allows track workers to get clear of the structure as a train approaches.

A viaduct in High Wycombe, where a refuge can be clearly seen with the gap protected by railings. Note the street furniture surrounding the structure.

A new signal fitted into a refuge on a viaduct. The signal is enclosed in the protective mesh as the line is being electrified. The mesh protects personnel working on the signal.

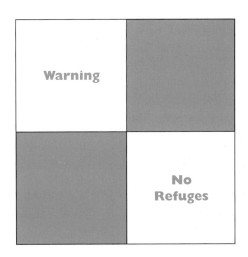

SAFETY RAILS

On some structures where parapets are low safety rails are added, especially in more recent times. The rails are usually tubes around 2in (50mm) diameter supported by stanchions set in the parapet coping stones. The stanchions can take several forms. Common is 'L' section steel around 3in (75mm) with each leg drilled to accept the rail, which is threaded through. An alternative stanchion is in cast iron

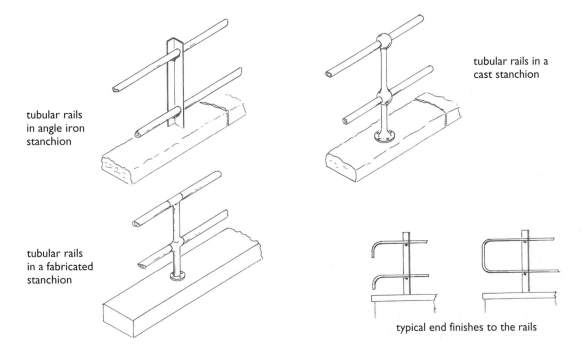

tubular rails in angle iron stanchion

tubular rails in a fabricated stanchion

tubular rails in a cast stanchion

typical end finishes to the rails

The parapets on bridge structure are usually finished with safety rails. They increase the height of the bridge without adding any significant weight or reducing visibility. Some common types are shown. On some early bridges the stanchion may be some old rail; notable in the west is the use of old bridge rail. The rails are generally finished with an end that repeats the vertical element of a stanchion.

having bulbs with holes to pass the rails through. Occasionally old rail may be used as supports – often this was old and worn bullhead rail. More modern bridges employ an all-tubular system similar to scaffolding, having junction pieces in the uprights for the horizontal members. The ends of the rails are often curved down and around, or the upper and lower rails may be joined in a semicircle or oval.

Tubular safety rails on one of the new Welsh Highland Railway bridges near Beddgelert.

Rails in an angle-iron structure cantilevered from the main girder.

Cast-iron stanchions carrying two rails on Ais Gill viaduct. The stanchions have feet that are bolted to the parapet capping stones.

Midford viaduct on the old Somerset and Dorset line, with concrete stanchions supporting the rails.

Angle-iron stanchions with three rails. These are cemented into the parapet capping stones.

ADDITIONS AND REPAIRS TO STRUCTURES

Overhead electrification supports rarely fit bridges and viaducts that date from original railway construction. One solution is to bolt the uprights to the sides of the structure. Another is to introduce spaces by the partial demolition of the existing structure.

Crossley Viaduct about 1.5 miles (2.4km) north-east of Congleton. The catenary wires are carried on portal frame girders that are fixed into gaps in the parapet.

Girderwork attached to side of a viaduct at Castlefield, Manchester, awaiting the installation of the overhead wires.

Besides the physical changes imposed on a structure as the railways have developed, time also has had its effects. Stonework is often locally replaced by brick, often but not always, by engineering blue brick. Increasing loads on a structure can cause it to move. Walls may begin to bulge or the footings may require underpinning. Evidence of this may be seen by the use of internal tie-bars pulling the structure in on itself. The load-spreading plates and nuts show on the surface. A modern repair may be the use of rock

bolts to help stabilize a wing wall. Steelwork has to be patched due to corrosion. A drastic repair may be the addition of a second or jack arch within an arch to relieve loads. This may not be a subsequent addition but a necessity imposed during construction.

Gabions, wire cages filled with broken stone, are built up like large bricks let into the slope. They are also used at the bottom of an embankment slope as a retaining wall, often if the slope is showing some instability. Gabions can also be used like large stone blocks to reinforce structures.

The wing wall of this bridge has been patched with engineering bricks. Though not blue brick, these are still harder than the bricks for domestic use. Blue bricks have been used in the corner between the wing wall and the spandrel face. The reasons for the patching are not now clear.

Marple viaduct over the River Goyt, carrying the Manchester–Sheffield line, with one arch showing a substantial repair in brick. In close-up, the repair suggests the bulk of the facing of the spandrel that has been replaced, as some of the original facing stones remain in the brickwork.

Just a little further along the line from Marple viaduct the railway crosses the Peak Forest Canal, where the abutments of the girder bridge have had extensive tie-bars inserted. These tie-bars are tensioned, pulling the stonework in. Some are square to the stonework and others at an angle. The angled ones appear to have the tie-bars parallel to the canal.

Looking similar to tie-bars, these are rock bolts reinforcing the lower part of a retaining wall with a roadway above. On the opposite side of the wall there is no evidence of anything similar.

This is a girder bridge carrying a road over the railway at Bradford on Avon. It is clear that it has suffered some distress, with four patches this side at least, and extensive corrosion. The close-up of the girder shows the patches and deep corrosion in more detail. There is potential here as an example of exceptional weathering on a model.

ABOVE AND RIGHT: *This is an example of a 'bridge protection beam', here over the A37 highway, near Lydford, Somerset. Devices like these are erected to protect the bridge structure from over-height loads on road vehicles. Judging from the loss of paint, it works well. The detail shows the substantial attachment to the bridge abutment.*

Similar to the protection beam, smoke deflectors were usually fitted under a steel bridge, which served to prevent direct contact of a steam locomotive's exhaust with the bridge structure. They were shallow, inverted troughs secured to the underside of the bridge. They would be a little longer than the width of the bridge, and may have been folded to produce the sides of the trough or fabricated. The fittings holding them to the structure were substantial, as they had to resist the force of the exhaust directed at them, sometimes quite closely. With the loss of steam on the railways, they have largely disappeared and may only be found on heritage sites.

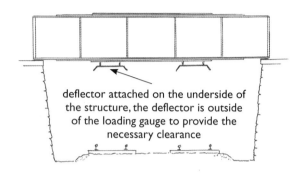

deflector attached on the underside of the structure, the deflector is outside of the loading gauge to provide the necessary clearance

Smoke deflectors used to be added under bridge structures to protect them from the sooty deposits: these deposits can be sulphurous and so generate acids that attack the steel or ironwork, and the accumulation of soot can hold water, so increasing the risk of corrosion. The plates can have a variety of shapes, the edges bent or curved down. The ends extend beyond the bridge structure and can be bent upwards for a short distance. Finding such structures is difficult on the modern railway, but some heritage lines retain them.

Here gabions are being used to reinforce a small occupation bridge on an access road to a farm. They have been built up in a double thickness, up to, and on both sides of, the arch supporting and reinforcing the spandrels. This is the current solution to long-standing problem of a bridge that originally never anticipated the passage of ever heavier agricultural machinery.

Gabions reinforcing the embankment beside Bryn-y-Felin bridge in the Aberglaslyn Pass near Beddgelert. Note they have been placed with a slight batter, leaning towards the embankment.

Jack arches built to support the deck and stabilize a pier when there is a failure. The failure can be due to either overloading the deck or a loss of footing to a pier causing a collapse. In this case it was the latter during construction.

CHAPTER FOUR

MODEL BRIDGES

COMMERCIAL SOURCES

There are a number of commercially available bridges from several different manufacturers both in the UK and overseas. The majority of these are for the smaller scales N and 00/H0 but there are some for 0 and larger scales too. Manufacturers to look for are, historically, Triang and Hornby Dublo and today,

Hornby, Bachmann, Dapol, Peco, Roco and Atlas and others. There are specialist manufacturers for bridges in the larger scales that are made from riveted aluminium section, ideally suited to the garden.

Peco manufacture a number of different bridge types that can be used in several scales. The series of pictures show them in use on some of their Pecorama layouts.

Several of the bridges in the Peco range that can be seen incorporated into layouts at Pecorama, Beer. This is an excellent location to see how these products can be used on a layout. The first picture in the series shows a bow plate girder used in a mainline location. The second shows a small bridge used for a narrow-gauge line. The third shows a pair of truss girders being built into a new American line set-up in a typical American-type deck truss. The final picture shows their viaduct spanning a lower level railway scene.

An offering for the O Gauge modeller from Seven Mill Models, a 7mm version of one once produced by Hornby Dublo. It is cast in metal just like the original 4mm model. The finish reflects that model too.

MODELLED BRIDGES IN 7MM AND 4MM SCALE

The accompanying illustrations are of structures that grace several model railways around Britain. They have all been built from scratch, some in metal, some in plastic and other materials. On some, both photo-etching and laser-cutting processes have been used to great effect to ensure the uniformity of parts.

TOP RIGHT, ABOVE AND BOTTOM LEFT:
This is Barry Kelsall's model of Barmouth bridge over the Afon Mawddach estuary, Gwynedd. It faithfully follows the prototype except that it has been shortened in the southern wooden section and, like the original, the swinging span to clear the navigation no longer moves. The main spans and northern viaduct have been made from brass section and photo-etched parts; the southern viaduct is correctly made of wood. For uniform construction of the piers, they have been assembled in jig. Note the rusty finish, inevitable for a structure in seawater, and the detail of residual seaweed.

ABOVE AND TOP RIGHT: *A detail of Hassel Harbour Bridge from the layout of the same name built in 7mm:1ft by the Alsager Railway Association. It is a convincing assembly that is not iron and steel but, as shown by the early stages of construction revealing major parts, the arch girders have been laser-cut in ply, and other parts added. The lattice girders are plastic from the Plastruct range. The gusset plates are in brass and the rivets fixing them are pins.* MIKE SANT

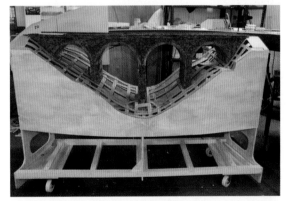

MIDDLE RIGHT: *A viaduct based on Ais Gill viaduct on Yeovil Model Railway Group's layout 'The Summit'. Its construction follows the description in Chapter 10. Its size means that for a portable layout this structure will be difficult to lift, so it has been built on its own wheeled baseboard structure. The scenery is in the early stages of construction, with the profile added in card strips and subsequently followed by squares of newsprint to surface it, then the scenic dressing.*

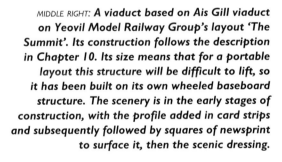

BOTTOM: *Swiss concrete structures squeezed into a valley on a loft layout.*

A series of bridges across a canal on Yeovil Model Railway group's layout 'Gas Works'. First is a straight plate-girder bridge; second, a bow plate-girder bridge; and, in the background, a straight plate-girder bridge with radiused ends. All are made in plasticard as described later. The layout can only be viewed from one side, so the backs of each structure have no detail.

A stone viaduct based on Hamwood Viaduct on the Somerset and Dorset line. It is built in plasticard as described in Chapter 10. Rather than brick, it uses embossed stone.

IN THE GARDEN

The accompanying pictures show bridges in the garden. Having the space allows for some ambitious structures. The following description is taken from the builder of the bridges who has taken an engineering approach, rather than a modelling one.

Garden railway bridges require a completely different approach and other methods of construction than those of indoor railways; they could be deemed as 'miniature civil engineering'.

Train-supporting bridges (as opposed to non-load bearing road-over type bridges) used in a garden will require far more strength than their indoor counterparts. Other factors to be taken into account for these types of bridges will be:

- Strength required.
- Type of material.
- Method of construction.
- Durability.

Strength required demands a number of factors to be considered, taking into account the weight of trains and the design/type of bridge construction, for example arches, suspension, girder and so on, but also other factors such as sparrows, seagulls, squirrels, cats, dogs, foxes, children, flying branches and maybe the odd earthquake!

The type of material to be used has to take into account factors such as:

- Practicality of the structure.
- A method of construction that is within the skill of the builder.
- Equipment available to manufacture.
- Cost of materials.
- Durability/resistance to corrosion.

Practicality is the ease of working with the material and the builder's familiarity with the techniques required to work the materials to be used.

Method of construction has to take into account the builder's skills for working with these materials and the ease or complexity of doing so.

As heavy-duty construction is used for these bridges, then a lot of heavier and different types of equipment may be needed, such as welding equipment, bending/folding equipment, heavier drilling

Bridging the 'other' garden railway' is one loosely based on the idea of an old Victorian 'Brunel style' iron bridge. The semi-elliptical arch is constructed from black steel, 10mm square section with a black steel 16mm × 3mm strip welded above and below, to form an 'I'-beam. The top main longitudinal support panelled beams are constructed from lightweight 1in square box section steel (old shop display stands use this type of material), with strips of 16swg steel welded to the top and bottom, and welding rod brazed vertically to form 'construction panels'. The fancy scroll ironwork bracing between the elliptical I-beam and top beam is constructed from steel sheet edged with welding rod brazed in place. The circular bracings are sections cut from various sized tubes and welded in place. 18mm (0.7in) ply forms the main deck, covered with torch-on roofing felt, the track being pinned directly on top. Wiring for the bridge is fed through a sealed hole through the deck with a weatherproof plug that plugs into a socket in the ring main bus, which feeds the supply to the railway. This bridge is constructed as a gate to enable access to the garden and allows running on the ground-level 5in gauge railway – often described as 'a gate with a railway on top'. GEOFF BYMAN

The second bridge, once again made from black steel, is based on the Victoria Bridge on the Severn Valley Railway. The fascia panels have been machined on a CNC miller from aluminium plate. The main low-arch span I-beam is once again constructed in three parts. But this time the centre of the I-beam is a deeper design and is made from 19mm × 3mm black steel positioned vertically with 16mm × 3mm black steel strips welded either side. The beam joint flanges are represented, once again, with welding rod brazed in place. The top main longitudinal beam is constructed from 25mm equal angle iron with a 16mm × 3mm black steel strip drilled and milled with a simple homemade cutter to represent an ornate wrought-iron edging. The fascia panels, milled from aluminium plate, are loosely based on those of the North Bridge at Halifax. Once

again, the deck is constructed of ply, again covered with torch-on roofing felt. The bridge is supported on two step-down 'Z plates', suitably pegged for alignment, with threaded height adjusters, and an elongated hole in the bridge that fits the peg, allowing for expansion. The 'Z' plates are screwed to the tops of the base boards either side of the bridge, allowing for any movement of the boards (height-wise) due to humidity and temperature changes, thus keeping the bridge perfectly aligned at all times. This method of location allows for both quick alignment and removal of bridges (simply lift out) at any time. GEOFF BYMAN

This is a completely freelance design of semi-hyperbola shape and of suspension principle. The main arch I-beam is constructed as the bridge shown at the top of page 71. The top cross-bracing beams are also fabricated from black steel. The main longitudinal deck side-support beams are once again constructed from lightweight square hollow section, as per the bridge at the top of page 71. The four vertical support pillars, below the main platform at each end, are made from steel rod with the end bosses machined, in steel, on the lathe. The suspension wires are made from welding rod with the top fixings made from car-brake tubing, swaged with single flared ends, brazed in place. The deck fixings at the lower end of the suspension wires are machined from aluminium, once again on the CNC Miller, in two halves and bolted together using stainless steel nuts and bolts. These fixings are machined on the inside to fit over pre-pressed half loops at the lower end of the suspension wire to allow the bolts to pass through. The decking this time is made from 9mm thick UPVC, screwed into place on the inside extension of the lower part of the steel strip of the main longitudinal support beams. The UPVC is suitably scored on the top face to represent wooden planking, with the track screwed down every eight or ten sleepers using brass screws. The change to UPVC, provided it is adequately supported, is proving to be far better than plywood with regards to durability. All my other bridges will eventually be converted to this method of decking. The bridge is supported at the base of the hyperbola beam and under the main deck support beams at either end, once again on stainless steel support plates, pegged in the same manner as the bridge at the bottom of page 71. GEOFF BYMAN

equipment and the like, than the average modeller is accustomed to.

These bridges will be larger than the indoor model, so their cost is a big consideration. Materials such as aluminium, galvanized steel or reinforced plastic may be considered for durability reasons; the cheaper option of black steel may often be the answer in these cases.

Durability has to take into account the local climate, especially the sun, as well as corrosion resistance and resistance to deformation due to humidity and temperature changes.

All the bridges are painted with Hamerite paint,

which, so far, has lasted five to six years between paintings. All lining is carried out with Hamerite gold paint, suitably thinned with the cellulose thinners, applied with brush and lining pens.

With all exterior bridges of this sort, extremely fine detail is not required, as usually the bridges are viewed 'from a distance'. As the builder says, 'It is just the overall impression that counts'.

SOME 4MM BRIDGES

This is a selection of bridges from 4mm layouts seen at exhibitions around the country and at home.

Two small bridges on Yeovil Model Railway Group's 4mm EM layout 'South Junction'. Both are made in plasticard. They are some of the first structures I made, it seems, a long time ago.

This is the very first viaduct I made. It too is on Yeovil Model Railway Group's layout 'South Junction'. This too has ply trackbed supporting plasticard details.

Two bridges on Cliff Parsons' layout 'The Gresley Beat'; a layout that captures the environs of the East Coast main line on the approaches to King's Cross. The first bridge has a fine mixture of masonry and steel structures in combination with a variety of heights to be bridged. The second is a box-girder bridge. The structure in this type of bridge is within a decorative cover, here exemplified by the bright colour scheme.

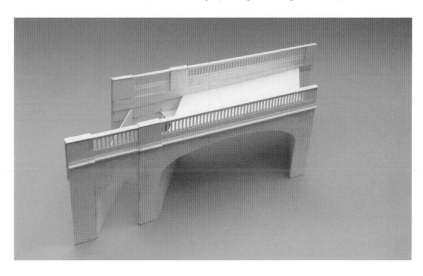

A bridge in the raw. This is intended for a layout by Malcolm Young featuring Sydney Gardens, Bath, here in raw plasticard. The balustrade has been laser-cut; hand-cutting such a feature may not produce such a regular finish.

DAVID SPENCER

A viaduct and bridge on the late Tom Harland's S4 layout 'Bramblewick'. Set in the north-east, the stonework captures the area very well.

A classic model viaduct: the Brunel timber span by Guy Williams on the Pendon Dartmoor layout.

CHAPTER FIVE

MODELLING – MATERIALS, TOOLS AND TAKING MEASUREMENTS

MATERIALS

My preferred material for structures is plastic sheet, plain and embossed. The plain sheet comes in thicknesses from 0.010 to 0.080in, usually in white or black, though some colours are available. The embossed sheet comes in a variety of stone finishes and different brick courses. There are a goodly number of plastic sections: I-beams, angles and solid sections that work well with the sheet material too. Again these come in a variety of sizes. There is advantage in using the plastic sections as they replicate steel engineering sections.

Butanone adhesive – this is a 500ml bottle rather than the usual smaller bottles; I tend to use a lot. Beside it is the 'working' bottle. This is set in a block of MDF as an anti-spill device. It also serves to store the brushes used to apply the adhesive.

For me, the speed of assembly using the solvent adhesives like MEK or Butanone outweighs the use of card and paper with their slower adhesives. Some prefer the latter, but I am an impatient modeller. The examples that follow later all utilize plastic in one form or another.

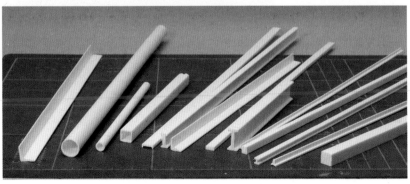

Plasticard sheets in brick, plain and stone embossed. These can be sourced from several manufacturers: large, plain sheets in a variety of thicknesses come from Slater's Plastikard, while a variety of sections are available from Evergreen and Plastruct.

TOOLS

Some of the tools I use are from an earlier engineering career, such as dividers, squares and rules. These will help with the accuracy of your work if used correctly. Use rules with divisions engraved into the surface, not etched – you are able to pick up the grooves with the dividers with greater accuracy than if the divider is resting on an etched line. Similarly, the groove enables you to transfer a dimension to the surface more accurately. Using the rule, its edge brings the scale into direct contact with the surface.

In conjunction with these tools, some drawing instruments can help. White plasticard will accept an HB pencil, so parts can be marked out before cutting. The illustration shows set squares and both an ordinary compass and a beam compass or trammel. The latter is used for drawing large circles.

Basic drawing kit for circles and lines: compasses, trammel and set squares. No pencil!

Another essential is the cutting mat. This provides a surface that supports the work and as a blade breaks through will not deflect it as might a wooden surface.

I prefer scalpels for the majority of my cutting with occasional recourse to a Stanley knife for heavy cuts. Other craft knives may be your choice or one of the commercial plastic cutters often referred to as a 'scrawker'. These cut by scraping a groove into the

The basic measuring and marking out tools: dividers and rules. The rules should have engraved divisions so that measurements can be taken from them by setting the points of the dividers in the grooves. The dividers can also be used to cut circular lines in the plasticard. The set squares ensure right angles when marking parts out. In addition, a 12in (30.5cm) woodworking one is useful when working on large sheets.

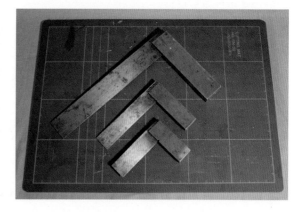

A Stanley knife and two scalpels; one is a No.3 handle with a straight blade and the other, less used, is a No.4 handle with curved blade. The latter is useful for a rolling cut into a corner. They are on a small cutting mat.

surface of the plastic sheet. If using a blade, it needs to be sharp. As blades blunt, then you are inclined to add more pressure to your cut, which will lead to blades breaking. This has the potential to not only damage what you are cutting, but yourself. A small saw is useful for cutting the larger plastic sections.

When using a blade, the edge of the cut throws up a small ridge of material from displaced material. This can be significant in thicker material. A 'scrawker' actually removes material, making a groove. This can be less accurate than a blade, especially if you cut the wrong side of the line.

To minimize the ridges it is only necessary to partially cut into the surface. The material can be snapped along the resulting groove. It even works around a curve. Take care when cutting, it is all too easy to leave finger tips over the edge of the rule in the path of the blade.

Curves can be cut with either dividers or a compass. The point of the dividers can be used to deeply scribe the curve. However, if this is a large radius, then the groove can enter at an angle leaving a bevelled edge to the parts you have cut out. This can be minimized if the cut is made from both sides. Finding the centre on the other side can be a challenge, so drilling a small hole through can help. On thick material the scribed line often needs assistance from a blade before the part can be snapped out.

Ordinary compasses or the beam compass can be used if the lead is substituted for a cutting tool. This

This shows the effects on plastic using different methods to cut it. A knife – Stanley or scalpel – will throw up a burr either side of the blade. This is because no material has been removed: it has been displaced to either side of the blade. Scoring with a point has a similar effect, even though some material is removed. This burr has to be removed either by scraping or shaving. The 'scrawker' removes material so creates a negligible burr. The homemade insert to my trammel and compass works the same way. In the compasses the groove will be angled.

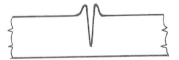

knife cut – burr thrown up each side of the blade

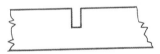

a 'scrawker' or the tool in the trammel – held vertical

scoring with a divider – similar burr

the scraping tool in compasses – angled

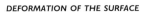

DEFORMATION OF THE SURFACE   *SCRAPED CUTS*

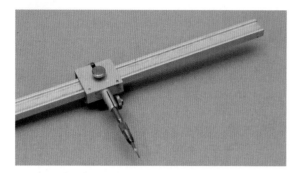

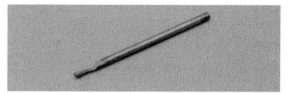

The beam compass or trammel fitted with a cutter instead of a pencil lead. A length of 1.5 mm diameter silver steel has been filed and ground to the shape shown. It acts as a scraper.

can be filed from some 2mm ($^5/_{64}$in) diameter silver steel. It is simply filed to make a thin scraping end. Even with this, when a large radius is cut with the compasses a bevelled edge can result; it is better used for small radii and the beam compass for the larger.

In addition to the knives for cutting out, other tools can be used for shaping and cleaning-up. A coarse, flat file, 10in (25cm) long or thereabouts can be used to shape blocks of plasticard. Another tool for shaping and cleaning up is a sheet of 180 grit wet and dry stuck to a piece of melamine-faced chipboard. Pieces are rubbed on to the abrasive surface to smooth them or to shape radii.

The Proxxon saw, showing some signs of use with plasticard dust over it. The blade guard has been lifted to show the blade. To one side is the fence to set the width of the cut. I usually set the distance with a rule between the blade and the fence, as it is more accurate than the scale along the front. The set of the blade has to be allowed for in the measurement. The plug is always out whilst I do this; no danger of switching on with fingers in close proximity.

Some tools are expensive but are particularly useful, especially if you contemplate modelling a lot of structures. Foremost is a small, circular saw. The model illustrated is made by Proxxon. It has a 58mm (2.25in) diameter saw. Saws come with a variety of teeth but the coarse one supplied with the machine works well with plasticard. The fence allows consistent widths to be cut. I use it for making strips as it is more accurate and consistent than marking out and cutting with a blade. The burrs produced tend to stick to the edge of the plasticard from frictional heating, especially if the material is forced through, but if the cut is made at the pace the blade feels happy with, then the burrs can be rubbed off with fingers and the edge cleaned by scraping a blade along the resulting corner. It will cut thicknesses from 0.030in (0.075mm) to 0.3in (8mm).

Another useful tool for making repetitive items is an American product: The Chopper from North West Short Line. It is available in the UK from several suppliers. A blade is pulled down on to plasticard strip and cuts it cleanly and square. The lengths can be set to suit. Apart from providing an end stop, a pair of guides allows different angles to be cut.

If working in the larger scales, then rivet detail can be prominent. A riveting tool that embosses the plasticard can be used to advantage. The one illustrated here has been with me for a time and is no longer in production. There are other varieties of these tools – one that produces rivets by positive hand pressure with a lever is best. Make sure it allows consistent spacing of the rivets by indexing. There are riveters that work by dropping a weight. They do not work on plasticard unless it is very thin.

The Northwest Shortline 'Chopper'. A single-bladed razor blade is attached to the handle that swings down to make a vertical cut in the plastic or wood. The blade is renewable. The two cutting guides/stops can be be clamped in appropriate positions. Cuts that are square or angled to the end can be made.

A modelling drill could be considered essential. Make sure it has a good speed control, especially one that has a slow speed of around 1,000 rpm or less. Drilling at high speed results in intense frictional heating and the plastic melts and builds up around the drill bit. A 1mm drill creates a 3mm hole! Other than drills, sanding drum can be used to shape components. For plasticard a coarse grit is better than a fine. Dental burrs can also be used to excavate holes in thicker plasticard and create surface texture.

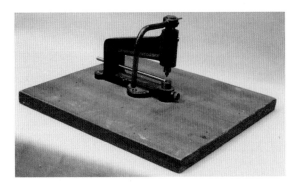

My riveting tool. Unfortunately no longer available, but others that use levers to impress the material over an anvil are available. The bar at the base sets the rivet distance from the edge. The anvil has an eccentric turning around the hole, which sets the pitch of the rivets determined by the distance of the circle from the hole.

An alternative riveting tool of the style I call a calibrated hammer. This one I made myself but there are commercial versions available. The weight is lifted to a set height, limited by the nuts on the studding, and then dropped to hit the nuts at the end and thus forcing the point into the material. There is no anvil or other setting device. The surface has to be marked for the rivet positions. The surface it is used on needs to be compliant in order for the rivet to be impressed. It is not particularly effective on plasticard over 0.020in thick.

The modelling drill with a sanding drum fitted. When using drills like this, keep the speeds low to reduce frictional heating when used on plasticard.

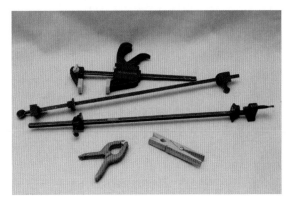

Various clamps, including a peg.

Finally, a selection of clamps is useful. There are spring clamps in various sizes, ratcheting clamps and miniature sash clamps available. Domestic washing pegs can be used too. Being wooden the ends can be shaped to suit a particular application.

TAKING MEASUREMENTS

In the best case a scale drawing of a structure can be used. These can be found in some publications and histories of lines. Some can be found in the National Railway Museum (NRM), though their archive is limited to railways of the North-East. Another source is the Archive of the Institution of Civil Engineers (ICE). An enquiry regarding your prototype may well get results. Other museums in the vicinity of your prototype may have drawings and photographs in their archives. I have found Network Rail to be singularly unhelpful.

Generally it is necessary to work from photographs with some limited dimensions. Taking these dimensions may be difficult or potentially dangerous. Never trespass on the railway. Even running a tape around the accessible part of a structure can put you in the path of road traffic.

Sometimes it is easier to work from photographs off-site. If you can take your own photos, then take them with a measuring pole in view.

The pole illustrated is a length of domestic waste-pipe. At the bottom it shows 6in (15cm) intervals and the remainder in 1ft (30cm) intervals. Use Imperial dimensions rather than metric as most structures were designed and built in those units. Your scaling will be in so many millimetres to the foot. The pipe was masked and sprayed black to create the divisions. As you can see it is a fraction over 6ft in length. This fits in the car comfortably.

Take photos with the pole both vertical and horizontal. Either prop the pole on the structure or have an assistant to hold it. The subsequent images can be scaled using the pole as a known dimension. There will be some inevitable inaccuracy due to the small sizes of the image you are measuring, but this should not be an issue. For instance, if you make a height 12ft 10in call it 13ft.

The measuring pole against my gatepost with bit of a lean. It helps for it to be as near as possible to the wall you need to measure.

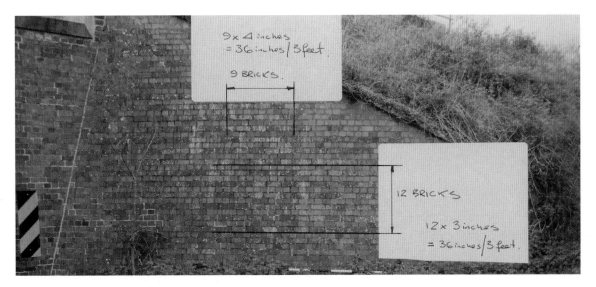

Counting bricks.

An alternative to the pole are the bricks in a structure. A brick measures 8.5 × 4 × 2.5in. Count the bricks and multiply, for vertical dimensions, by 3, or for horizontal dimensions, by 9 to give the measurement in inches. These numbers take into account the thickness of mortar. Mortar in structures, especially old ones, is thin by comparison with modern structures.

Stonework can be more difficult, especially if it is random stone. If at all possible, find a known dimension in the picture and use that.

SCALING FROM A PHOTO

Some draughting skills are needed to do this but it is not too difficult.

In the picture on p.82, the view is square to the bridge. Passing under it are two tracks. The trackwork can be used to provide the known dimension; the gauge of the track, 4ft 8½in, is not at first sight a helpful dimension. In the view it is difficult to resolve half an inch, so call it 4ft 8in. Multiply this by 3 and you get 14. You now have a known dimension of 14ft. So the track gauge can be transferred times three to form the basis of a scale particular to that photo.

A line is drawn across the top of the rails to provide a datum. The vertical corners are then defined and the horizontal at the bottom of the arch.

A scale is produced from the known dimension. A drawing board is helpful here but any flat surface will do. A line is drawn with the start point defined. Using dividers, take the track gauge from the photo and space it three times along the line. Mark the end. You now have a line that is 14ft long with respect to the photo. To find individual foot divisions proceed as follows:

1. From the start point of the line, draw a line at an angle above the 14ft line.
2. Set an arbitrary dimension on the dividers and walk off 14 divisions and mark them.
3. From the last division draw a line down to the last point along the 14ft line. If you have an adjustable set square, set the angle to match this line. Otherwise with two set squares, set the first on the line and, holding the second firmly, arrange it to slide down the second, keeping the lines parallel.
4. From each of the 14 divisions draw a line parallel to the first line down to the 14ft line.

This has now given 1ft intervals along the line, creating a scale. Dimensions can be taken from the photo and matched to the scale.

The bridge photo marked out defining the basic rectangle below the arch. From this the track gauge can be taken.

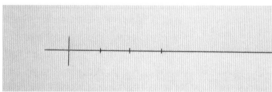

The track gauge in 4ft 8in intervals transferred to the base line; 3 × 4ft 8in equals 14ft.

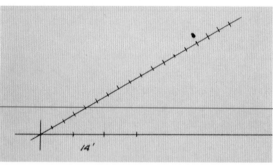

A line is drawn at an angle; this is arbitrary but should be around 30–45 degrees and is divided into fourteen parts. A nominal dimension is set for this division.

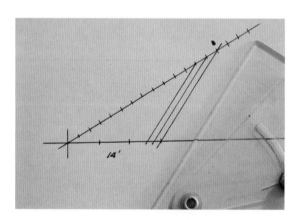

A line is drawn between the fourteenth division, marked with a spot and the last division on the horizontal line. The square is set to the same angle as the line, and from each division on the upper line a line is drawn to the horizontal line.

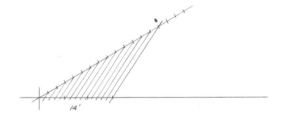

The horizontal line has now been divided into fourteen parts each equal to 1ft. Dimensions of less than 1ft can be estimated from the scale. In this case I would be happy down to 3in.

A simple way to draw an ellipse. The larger semi-circle is the width of the arch and the smaller the height. From the centre of the semi-circles draw a series of radial lines at 15-degree intervals. Where these lines intersect the larger semi-circle, drop vertical lines and on the smaller semi-

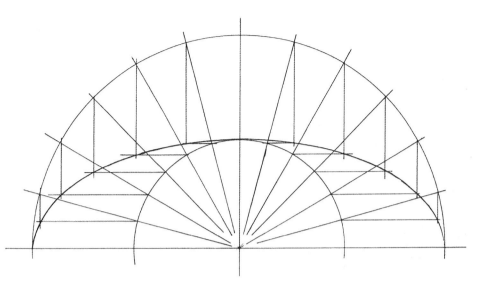

circle draw horizontal lines from the intersection. The points where the horizontal and vertical lines intersect define the ellipse. Join the points with a French curve.

The picture also shows an elliptical arch. The following is probably the simplest method of drawing an ellipse.

1. From the photo draw a rectangle to scale. The longest dimension is the width of the arch, the shortest the height.
2. Find the centreline of the arch dividing the span in two.
3. On the centreline at the bottom of the arch draw a semicircle whose radius is the height of the arch.
4. Repeat where the radius is the span of the arch.
5. Divide the semicircles every 15 degrees.
6. Where the angular divisions cut the inner semi-circle, draw horizontal lines.
7. Where the angular divisions cut the outer semi-circle, draw vertical lines to intersect the horizontal lines. The intersections are the points around the ellipse.
8. Use a French curve to join the points to create the ellipse.

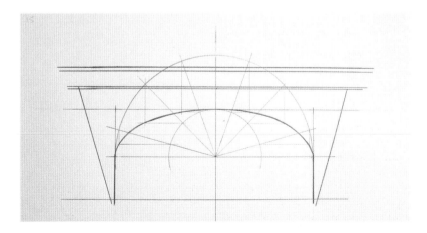

A drawing of the bridge scaled from dimensions taken from the photograph and the ellipse drawn on using those dimensions.

Table 1 Clearance dimensions for structures: overbridges

	Prototype	
Minimum clear opening for single line*	13ft 8in	4,166mm
Desirable clear opening for single line*	15ft 6in	4,724mm
Minimum clear opening for double line*	24ft 10in	7,569mm
Desirable clear opening for double line*	26ft 6in	8,077mm
Minimum clear opening for four lines with one 10ft (3m) space*	51ft 2in	15,596mm
Desirable clear opening for four lines with one 10ft 6in (3.2m) space*	53ft 6in	16,307mm
Minimum headway – above rail top	14ft 6in	4,420mm
Desirable headway – above rail top	15ft 0in	4,572mm
Minimum headway to clear overhead electrification wires – above rail top	14ft 8in	4,470mm
Desirable headway to clear overhead electrification wires – above rail top	15ft 8in	4,780mm
Width between parapets – major road	35ft 0in	10,668mm
Width between parapets – secondary road	25ft 0in	7,620mm
Width between parapets – private road	12ft 0in	3,658mm
Height of parapets	4ft 6in	1,220mm

*Note these dimensions may be further increased on the model where the bridge is over curved track to account for the tighter than prototype radii. The excessive swing of a locomotive and coaches could foul the structure if not checked.

Table 2 Clearance dimensions for structures: underbridges

	Prototype	
Headway – major road	16ft 0in	4,877mm
Headway – secondary road	15ft 0in	4,572mm
Headway – private road	14ft 0in	4,267mm
Width of roadways – as for overbridges		
Height of parapets	4ft 6in	1,312mm
Desirable width between parapets – single line	15ft 6in	4,724mm
Desirable width between parapets – double line	26ft 6in	8,077mm

CHAPTER SIX

A SIMPLE GIRDER BRIDGE

THE PROTOTYPE

This model is of a type that suits a light railway, a narrow gauge line or an industrial railway; it is simple and lightweight. The model is based on one that once crossed the River Dove at Tutbury, Staffordshire, which served the plaster works of J. C. Staton & Co. (more details can be found in

Railway Bylines, September 2009, Irwell Press). Nothing now remains but the piers, which were of several types: solid substantial ones at each end by the river banks and, not visible in the picture, continuing across the meadow of the flood plain; and a pair of lighter ones in the centre of the span. They appear to be a mixture of cast concrete and steel piles with a concrete cap.

Staton's own Peckett locomotive with BR 21T hopper wagons. The Peckett was built in 1949 and had the maker's number 2112. It was acquired for the plaster works in 1958 having previously served a brewery in nearby Burton on Trent. The wagons were originally built for coal traffic but have been found useful for the transport of the mined gypsum to the works to make the plaster. Gypsum is the product of evaporation of a salt-rich sea, often in a shallow lagoon. The wagons have tarpaulins in one view. This may be because they are full of gypsum and in the view without, empty.
CLIVE BAKER

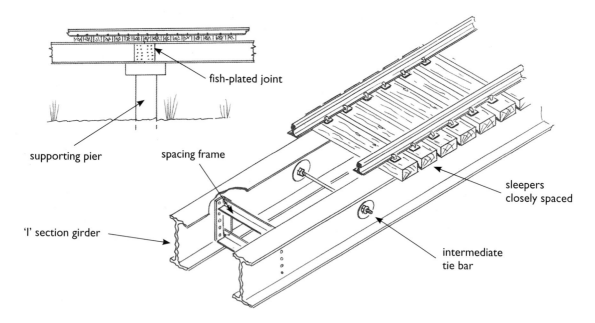

fish-plated joint

supporting pier

spacing frame

'I' section girder

sleepers closely spaced

intermediate tie bar

Elements of the simple girder bridge. Two 'I' section girders are laid side by side. The spacing matches the gauge of the track so varies between standard and narrow gauge. Every so often a small structure spaces the girders apart. Further intermediate tie bars space the girders between the structures. If the 'I' beams have to be joined they are fish-plated with plates in the web. The track I laid directly on the top of the beams. Wooden sleepers are closely spaced across the span to evenly distribute train loads into the structure. Some sleepers will be bolted to the top web of the beam to locate the track. The structure is supported on simple piers, often cast concrete.

THE MODEL

The model is not of the location illustrated. I have elected to shorten the span but show the same construction. Even so, modelled in 4mm:1ft, it is still a long bridge.

DEFINING THE SIZE

The first thing was to establish some ruling dimensions based on the Plastruct girder and the length of Peco track that crosses the bridge. One of the important dimensions is the spacing of the girders, which have to sit directly under the rails. The rail chairs nominally sit on the top flange of the girder. The track was measured to find the centreline of each rail; just a little bit wider than the gauge. This establishes the spacing of the spanning girders. It is worthwhile making a sketch and adding the dimensions to it.

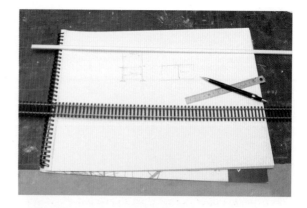

It is handy to have a sketchpad around when building any model. Making pictorial notes often helps to understand how something may go together. Here the track and a girder have been sketched and measured. The drawing does not have to be to scale but simply show the relationship between one part and other. The dimensions are noted to position the parts.

The girder was cut to two equal lengths. In this case it was from Plastruct $^5/_{16}$in I-section, 24in long. (Note that these sections also come in 12in lengths.)

Along the prototype there appeared to be cross-members every 10ft, indicated by small, vertical 'L' sections on the outer sides of the main girders. These were stepped out along the length by walking the dividers along the girder and making a pencil mark. An exact scale of 10ft did not divide into the length – this is not unusual, so some licence is needed. Accordingly it was divided into eight equal spaces; these were slightly less than the scale of 10ft. This not a great issue as the bridge has to 'look right' rather than be an exact scale model, exact scale being impossible when only photographic reference is available, as is often the case.

CUTTING OUT THE PARTS

Most of the components in this structure are from strip and sections. The strip has been mostly cut with the 'chopper' and the sections have been sawn.

ASSEMBLING THE BASIC STRUCTURE

Having marked out the spacer positions, they need to be made. The spacers were cut from Plastruct rectangular section. They were positioned and stuck to the girders.

The spaces for the cross-members are stepped out using the dividers. The point of the dividers can be pushed into the plastic to make a mark. This can be a problem, as it may disfigure the surface, so a small mark enhanced by a pencil is better.

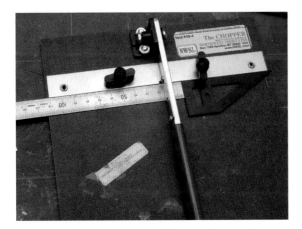

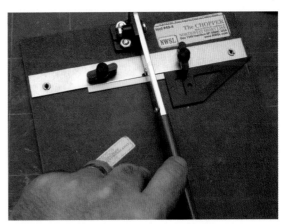

This is the chopper in use. First, the dimension is set. A small rule under the blade allows the stop to be located. The plastic strip is then pushed up to the stop and the blade pushed down to cut it. It is usually worth checking the first part cut off to ensure that the length is correct. Better to have one too short than twenty. You will note that the stop has an angle on it, this one at 30 degrees. There is a second one with a 45-degree angle. This allows other shapes to be made in more complex structures. If you do not have the advantage of a cropping tool, then the alternative is to walk the dividers along the strip, marking the distance with a small indentation. A sharp scalpel can be used to cut at these positions. There is the potential that the cut will not be square across the strip, so mark a line using a square or cut against the edge of the square. Usually it is sufficient to make a cut into the surface then snap the piece off.

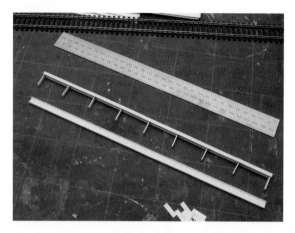

One of the girders with the spacers attached. Allow a little time for the joints to harden before proceeding.

The adhesive – a liquid solvent that softens the plastic – is applied with a small paintbrush. The parts to be joined are brought together and adhesive applied at the joint. The plastic softens and the two parts weld together. If too much adhesive is applied it can be removed by re-applying an empty brush, which will draw up the excess. Alternatively, since adhesive rapidly evaporates from the joint, blow on the area to further speed up evaporation, something that cannot be done with sticky tube cements. Bearing this in mind, adequate ventilation is needed to avoid a build-up of fumes.

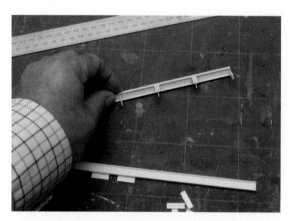

The capping strips are added before the second girder is fixed. It is usually sufficient to position the parts by eye, but sometimes a guide line can be scribed or pencilled on to the part as a reference.

As the adhesive is liquid it can run to places where it is not wanted, which is not a problem unless the area is handled. The softened plastic can pick up fingerprints.

Once secure, a capping strip is added to the top of each spacer to make a 'T'-section. This stiffens the structure and prevents the spacer translating sideways – in model and reality. At the ends the cap was positioned inside the ends, making an inverted 'L'. The cap here is a matter of conjecture as the pictures give no idea of the structure between the main girders. However, from observation on other structures such a detail is not unusual. Often detail can be inferred by looking at other structures doing the same job.

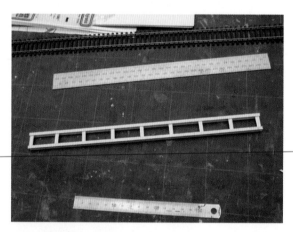

The capping strips are now in place and the second girder has been added. This is now a structure.

With all spacers in place the second girder is added, making a ladder structure. Check the spacers are square to each girder. At this stage it is best to set the structure aside to allow the adhesive to dry completely and the joints to harden. Other details can be prepared whilst this happens.

The girders show some indication of the internal structure along the outside, these being short, vertical 'L' sections. However, in 4mm there are no 'L'-sections small enough. General appearance is what matters, especially in the smaller scales. Instead the sections are represented by lengths of 1mm

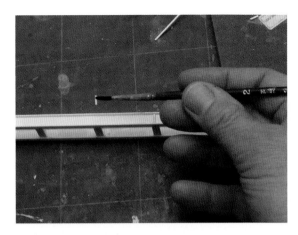

The small external strips being placed. They have been picked up on the adhesive paintbrush and floated into position. Final positioning before the adhesive dries is to push them into place with a scalpel. They were aligned with the inner cross-member by eye.

square styrene cut to fit on the girder web opposite the cross-members. These were positioned by picking them up with the paintbrush wet with adhesive and placing them on the side of the girder. This will tack them in position allowing them to be pushed into the correct position with tip of a scalpel. Alignment by eye is usually good enough. Once in the correct place, add a little more adhesive to be sure of a good fix.

OTHER DETAILS

Riveted fishplates are added to the side of the girders. These are positioned at one third of the span, to create an apparent joint in the girder.

To make these fishplates, rivets were embossed

A riveted fishplate stuck on at one-third of the span.

into 0.020in thick plasticard. The spacing of the rivets is set to a scale 6in apart along the length and 9in apart in the vertical. These dimensions were chosen as they 'looked right'. Adding the fishplates completes the basic bridge structure.

The tool I have uses positive pressure to form the dome of the rivet on an anvil. There are similar machines on the market that work in the same way. One form of rivet embosser that is available will not give a satisfactory result and that is the type that uses a small weight dropped down a shaft to apply a 'calibrated' hammer blow to the material. This does not have sufficient force to make a significant rivet in styrene sheet.

These pictures show my tool in use. It is easier to make small items like these fishplates on a larger sheet and then cut them out. Working on a large sheet is easier than trying to do it on the finished-size item. There is much more to hold on to. An alternative to embossing the rivets is to use one of the Slater's Plastikard sheets with embossed rivets, though the spacing may not always be suitable.

A recent innovation comes from America: three-dimensional transfer rivets. These are resin shapes printed on to decal film. A whole range of sizes and spacing is available. They are applied in a similar manner to a waterslide transfer. The company website has instructional videos showing them in use (http://www.archertransfers.com/SurfaceDetailsMain.html).

Another detail that could have been added is a pipe attached on one side. This can be seen in the prototype photos and appears to be on the downstream side. In times of flood, in this position it would be less likely to be damaged by debris being swept downstream.

MAKING THE PIERS

The bridge now needs its supports. The prototype ones were cast in concrete and also in steel fabrication and concrete. At the river bank there are more substantial examples: one lozenge shaped and the other ribbed. One wonders why they are not the same.

A simpler version is to use cylindrical uprights and a nominally rectangular lintel – rather like parts of Stonehenge.

The columns of the piers were cut from Plastruct tube. Using the dividers to set the length, a series of marks were scribed around the circumference of the tube. These have to be fairly close together to create a near continuous line.

The lintel on top of the piles comes next. This was laminated from three thicknesses of 0.080in plasticard. The circular saw is useful for cutting this thickness of material. Strips the width of the lintel were first sawn, then these strips cut to length.

With tubes and strips you now have a kit for the piers.

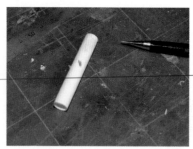
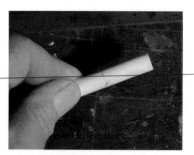

Using the dividers to mark the tube in preparation to cutting to length. To help make these marks show, especially on a white background, scribble over the line with an HB pencil, dampen a finger and rub the pencil mark into the groove. This trick can also be used on sheet material too.

Use a small square to guide the scalpel along the line. Having created a deeper score, cut around it again with the point of the scalpel, then simply snap off the length of tube.

TOP LEFT, ABOVE AND BELOW: **Here I am using the circular saw to cut 0.080in plasticard. The width is set between the blade and the fence. The set on the blade has to be allowed for, so ensure the measurement is taken from a tooth that faces towards the fence. It is advisable to disconnect the saw from the electrical supply when setting up the cut – just in case!**

ABOVE: **A set of parts ready for assembly. Making sets of parts like this is only a step away from buying a kit and then assembling it. It is just you making the bits, not a kit supplier.**

The three laminations show their edges, these need to be lost so the assembly was rubbed across a sheet of 180 grit wet and dry abrasive paper. Unless the parts are seriously out of register then this usually takes only a few strokes.

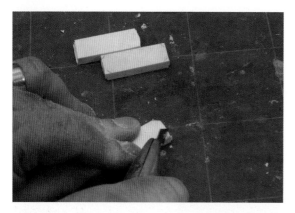 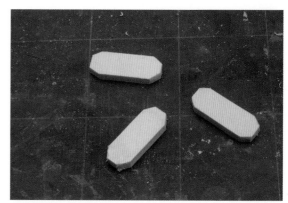

A small chamfer was added to the ends of the lintel. This was cut with the Stanley knife, though if you are confident with the power saw the ends can be cut with that, but this has to be done freehand as the fence cannot be used. The knife-cut ends were finished with a file.

Three lintel parts are laminated together and adhesive is applied to each surface to be joined. On thicker plasticard like this they can be joined immediately but on thinner material it is sometimes better to allow the adhesive to dry a little, leaving the surface tacky. Once the adhesive has dried, the edges are cleaned up using the wet and dry board. The chamfer at the ends was made by trimming the corner by cutting then finishing with a file.

The columns can now be added to the lintels. When adding a component like this with no distinct location, it is advisable to position them and mark the location before gluing. You can check for symmetry before fixing.

Once secure the piers are added to the bridge: one each end and one in the middle. This completes the basic bridge structure.

INSTALLING THE BRIDGE

To illustrate the installation, I prepared a scenic section with a river to be spanned. The bridge was

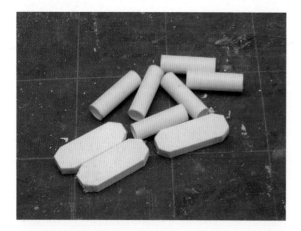 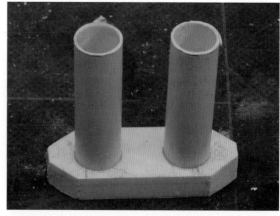

A set of parts ready for assembly. The locations for the columns were first marked on each lintel. The columns were lined up by eye before marking the positions with a pencil. Once happy with the positions, apply the adhesive. Using a liquid adhesive means it can be applied without disturbing the parts if applied with care.

offered up to this to check the fit. At this stage the scenery is 'in the raw', lacking a completed surface and greenery. I do not propose to describe this, as suitable methods can be found in Tony Hill's book *Creating Realistic Landscapes for Model Railways* also published by Crowood.

CHECK THE LOCATION

Unlike the prototype, where earthworks are excavated to accept a structure, the railway modeller often places the structure in position first and then adds the scenery later. In this case a river is nominally located between two banks and the earthworks are completed to fit the model.

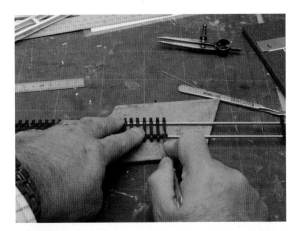

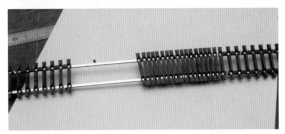

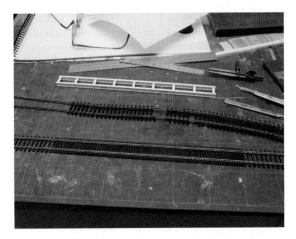

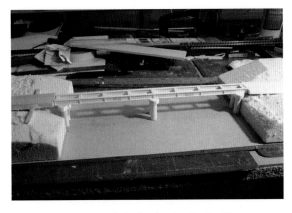

Here the position of the bridge is checked between the banks and the trackbed. The structure has only been placed at this stage, fixing comes later.

PREPARING THE TRACK

For this type of bridge the sleeper spacing is reduced from its nominal spacing. You can see in the prototype photos that the sleepers are not spaced but sit next to each other. The track used in this instance is from Peco. To close up the spacing, the webs spacing the sleepers need to be cut away. As result of closing up the sleepers, the rail at the end of the length of track ends up without sleepers. I used a second-hand donor length of track to provide the additional sleepers – the sleepers were salvageable but the rail was somewhat bent.

The webs between the sleepers on the underside of the track have to be removed for the sleepers over the bridge. A sharp knife is used to slice through them close to the sleeper. Several blades may be necessary as the blade blunts when it is stopped by the rail. As the web is removed and the sleepers closed up, you can see the developing gap in the track. Keep comparing the length of closed-up sleepers with the bridge span. Once enough sleepers have been moved, additional sleepers with webs from the donor track are slid down the rails each end to top up the section of track with sleepers at normal spacing.

FINISHING-OFF

At this stage you now have all the parts to complete the installation. Now is a good time to paint both the bridge and the track.

For the bridge deck I used aerosol grey acrylic primer from Halfords, part of their range of motor car finishing paints. This is the basic colour and when dry, a darker grey was dry-brushed into certain areas to accentuate the detail. A rusty finish was then applied in corners and along the bottom of the girders. The piers were finished to represent concrete.

The track has been finished in 'Sleeper grime' from the Railmatch range. This is simply a basic overspray to colour the track. The rail and chairs have then been brush painted with Humbrol enamel matt 'Rust'.

With the scenery nominally finished, the bridge was offered up again to complete the installation. Parts of the bank had to be cut away to accept the piers and a further check of the bridge fit made.

The ends of the trackbed need to be terminated to prevent the ballast falling down the bank. The prototype pictures offered no help here so I have guessed that there would be some form of retaining wall. The

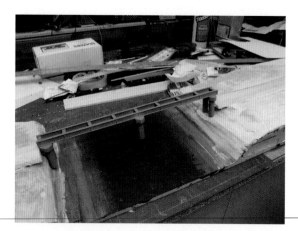

The bridge is offered up to the completed river banks. Holes are cut to allow the pier columns to sit in them. Fitting a structure into the ground is far more realistic than sitting them on the ground and leaving a gap between the structure and the ground, a feature seen all too often on models.

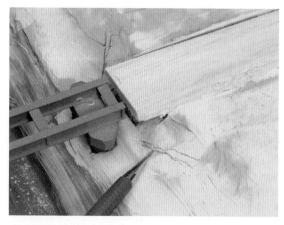

The bridge fitted next to the trackbed. The space is used to determine the retaining wall.

Here the bridge is now sitting in the ground. Clearly the trackbed needs some finishing at the end as it sticks into space.

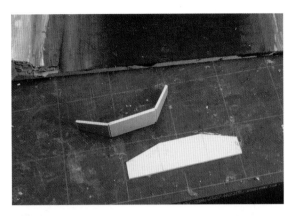

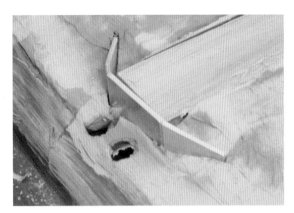

From the dimensions of the end of the trackbed, a piece of 0.080in plasticard has been cut and folded to make the basis of a retaining wall. It has been made deep enough to sit in the ground. The folds have been made by scoring the surface and bending the ends. For this item the aim is not to get the plasticard to break on the score, though if it does that is not the end of the world!

The retaining wall has been offered to the end of the trackbed and its position pencilled in. A slot has then been cut to receive it.

size was measured from the model and parts cut from 0.080in plasticard. The parts were offered up to the banks and their positions marked so that cuts could be made to sink them into the ground.

The retaining walls were completed with a layer of brick plasticard and capping strips on the wing walls.

They were then glued in position leaving the wall a sleeper thickness above the trackbed. The wall has to be as high as the top of the sleeper to form the support to the ballast that will be applied later.

With the retaining walls in place, the bridge was prepared for installation. It is not possible to pin the track to the deck as is usual on a baseboard, so I have used double-sided tape along the tops of the girders.

With the tape in place the bridge can be stuck into the scene. PVA adhesive was applied to the base of

The strips of double-sided tape have been applied to the tops of the girders. The tape as supplied is too wide so needs to be trimmed; to make trimming easier, align one edge of the tape along the inside edge of the girder to give an overlap of tape on the outside edge. Once both girders have the tape applied, turn the assembly upside down on to the cutting mat and trim the excess off with a sharp blade, using the outside edge of the girder as a guide.

The bridge set in place. An advantage of hollow piers is that adhesive (wood working pva) can be put inside and as the bridge is placed it runs down and makes an invisible joint with the surface they sit on. Note the large kitchen scale weight holding the assembly in place whilst the adhesive dries. At this stage it is often better to leave the work for a day or so whilst the glue dries.

the piers – an advantage here is having tubes because the glue can be put inside and, once in place, runs down and secures the bridge without an obvious fillet. Whilst the glue cured, a weight was set on the bridge to hold it down.

Where the piers are set in the banks, the holes were made good around them using a mixture of household filler coloured with the same paint that colours the banks; I use artist's acrylics. A portion can be squeezed into the filler and mixed in to make a paste with a little water.

Before fixing the track, paint it. To secure the track, the covering of the tape is removed and the closed-up sleeper section is lined up on the bridge. Once aligned, press it down to stick. The remaining track is pinned to the trackbed/baseboard. Further scenic dressing and ballast can then be added to complete the installation. You will note how the little retaining wall works to hold back the ballast.

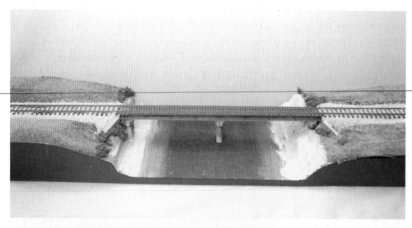

The completed bridge is now spanning the river. A little undergrowth serves to soften sharp edges. Some rust along the girders and dirt on the pier adds some age.

CHAPTER SEVEN

A TRUSS-GIRDER BRIDGE

THE PROTOTYPE

This model is a simple truss-girder bridge. It is similar to some of the new bridges on the rebuilt Welsh Highland Railway (WHR). However, the railway that this model carries is standard, rather than narrow gauge and is destined for a layout I am making.

THE MODEL

The main difference between the model and those of the WHR is that I have used a longitudinal baulk to support the rails, each supported by a longitudinal girder on cross-girders. The WHR bridges have a series of longitudinal girders allowing sleeper-supported track. I have also braced the trusses from extended girders; the trusses are thin on the model. A similar truss in reality would require the bracing because the loading tends to bend the main members in the plane of the truss, but lacking lateral stiffness the truss would translate sideways – bracing prevents that.

THE MATERIALS

The foundation of the bridge is truss girders from the Peco range of accessories. Though intended for 4mm scale they are adaptable for other scales, in this instance 7mm. The remaining parts are from the Plastruct range of sections and plasticard in different thicknesses. The girders and sections have to be sized to be in proportion for the scale, which means something at least a scale foot or more deep for the principal supporting parts. In 7mm this begins to show how light the trusses actually are, so some consideration has to be made as to how they may be made to look more substantial.

CONSTRUCTION

SETTING OUT THE LEADING DIMENSIONS AND MAKING THE BASIC DESIGN

As before, a scale drawing was made defining the leading dimensions for the cross-section of the

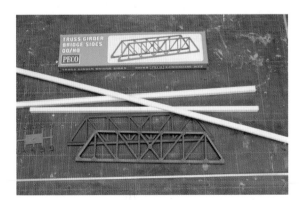

The principal components of the bridge: the Peco trusses and Plastruct sections, and the rail and its supporting chairs are shown. The rail chairs are from the C&L/Exactoscale range. This manufacturer also provides similar components in 4mm scale.

Measuring a typical item of rolling stock that will eventually cross the bridge. The dimension used was 80mm (3in). The coach is an ex-Hull and Barnsley four-wheel All third Brake, now pressed into light railway use.

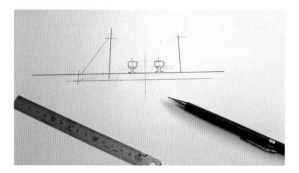

The drawing of the bridge cross-section – it only needs to be lines, not fully detailed. The inside edges of the trusses are defined and their height. The cross-girders are drawn, but only as much as is needed to provide the dimension to locate the side supports. On top of these are timber baulk-supporting girders, and on top of these the baulk.

bridge. This is the important set of dimensions, as a train has to pass between the trusses. To be certain, measure a typical item of rolling stock that will be using the bridge.

LONGITUDINAL MEMBERS

The longitudinal members are set by the length of the two trusses end to end. The length was made plus 1 scale foot to allow it to protrude beyond the seat on the abutment. The plastic sections used for these are too short so require joining.

Once the joints were set and solid, the plastic has to be made to look like wood. To do this the surface is abraded with coarse wet and dry (emery) paper. As this was a 7mm model, I used 60 grit – finer grit will suit smaller scales. Tear a corner of the wet and

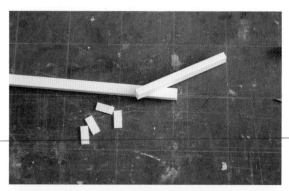

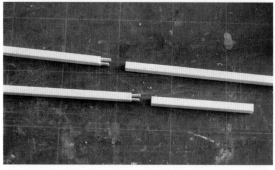

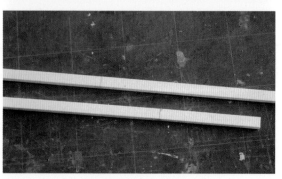

The 'timber baulk' is a hollow rectangular section. This allows it to be joined by small, plastic fishplates stuck inside the tube. The pictures show the successive stages of making the joint.

The tube and the fishplates: these are cut from 0.040in plasticard to fit the wider side of the tube.

The fishplates fixed in one side of the tube.

The tubes joined – the joints shown by the dirty lines. The unequal joint comes from the economical use of materials. A complete length required a short addition. The length that had the short piece cut from it had a longer part added to make its new complete length.

Drawing the wet and dry along the baulk. Always pull the paper down the length: in this case the left hand holds the tube and the right drags the wet and dry to the right, scoring the surface while keeping the component in tension. If the movement is reversed, compressing the part, you will probably buckle or bend the part.

A close-up of the roughened surface. The slight hairiness is not an issue – it can be left or the surface brushed with a suede brush. The wire bristles will remove the hairs and can further enhance the wood-grain effect. The final finish will be in the painting.

dry from its sheet, as a whole sheet is too unwieldy. This is then simply drawn along the surface of the plastic roughening it. The tiny scores become the surface effect of wood grain.

The timber baulk is now ready to receive the rails. I have used a system by C&L/Exactoscale that uses individual chairs to support the rail. Normally the chairs are fixed to a sleeper. The chairs used are 'bridge chairs'; these have a different footprint from a normal chair, even allowing for the different types of chair from different railway companies for running rail. They are specifically designed for the purpose they are being used for here, that is to support rail on a bridge longitudinal baulk.

The rail was prepared to receive the chairs by cutting to the appropriate length. In this case each rail across the bridge comprises 33ft (10m) lengths. This length of rail is an older standard, long super-seded today, but this bridge is intended to be used in a period when such lengths were still common. Notwithstanding, the rails are not three actual lengths but a single one of a scale 90ft (27m) and the two rail joints are made by cutting through the head of the rail to suggest the joint. The cut is made with a fine saw.

The chairs are fed on to the rail noting that the keys (the wooden wedges that hold the rail in the chair) face in alternating directions. The movement of a train on the rail tends, depending on its direction of travel, to drive the rail into or out of the chair relative to the key. By alternating them on what is a bi-directional track, movement is minimized.

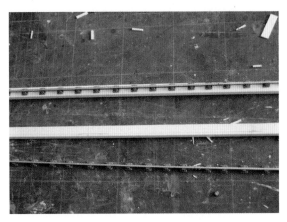

The chairs have been fed on to the rail and nominally spaced. The top rail has been placed on to the timber baulk. The lower rail awaits location. To aid positioning, a pencil line has been drawn to help set the edge of the chair from the edge of the baulk. On this rail, a rail joint cut can be seen and a cosmetic fishplate.

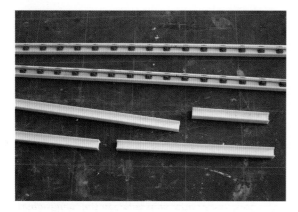

The completed timber baulks with rails with the girder parts waiting fixing.

The chairs are spaced as they would be if on a conventional sleeper, 2ft 7in (78cm) apart. This still leaves a portion of rail beyond the timber baulk that will require conventional chairs and sleepers.

The rails are secured to the timber baulk with a small amount of adhesive applied to each chair. It is important that constant checks are made to keep the rail straight and at a constant distance from the edge of the baulk. Once the adhesive is dry, then the baulk supporting girder can be added underneath.

Once again, the 'H' girder section as supplied is too short and so the length of each is made up. Unlike the baulk tube, a fishplated joint is not neces-

sary. A simple butt joint will give the appearance of a continuous girder. A clean, square end is required for this.

The girder is stuck to underside of the timber baulk ensuring the vertical web of the girder is on the centreline.

CROSS-MEMBERS

The completed parts were set aside whilst the cross-members were prepared from 'I'-section girders. Four short and four long cross major girders were needed. The dimensions were taken from the previously prepared sketch.

The cross-members of the bridge are set out by the trusses. At each end, and under each vertical member of the truss, there has to be a cross-member. Some of these cross-members are longer than others for the side supports. The truss design means that there cannot be a support at every vertical. The end verticals need one. The loading on the bridge will cause the maximum deflection of the truss in the middle; therefore, the remaining side supports are placed on the two middle verticals.

In addition to the major cross-members, smaller ones are needed between the longitudinal girders; these represent the ties between them. These members need to be nested inside the flanges of the longitudinal girders. First, the distance between

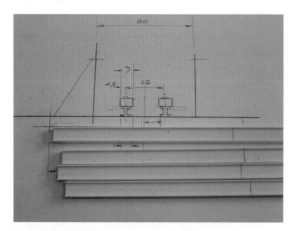

The 'I'-section girder marked ready for sawing to length. Sawing this material will produce a better cut than any attempt with a knife.

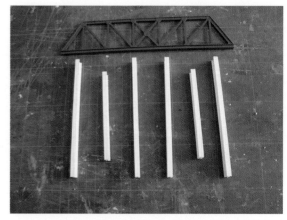

Here the cross-girders are laid in their nominal positions relative to the verticals of the truss. The two outer, short ones are missing in this view.

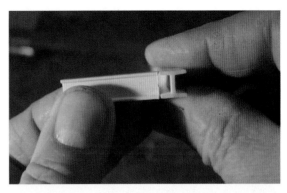

This shows the general set-up of the track parts relative to the rule. As the girders are symmetrical, the dimension can be taken from one flange edge to the other. This is easier than trying to measure between each vertical web. The dimension is 32mm (1.25in). One of two track gauges serves to hold the parts in the correct relative positions.

This shows the relationship between the longitudinal girder and the cross-piece. It can be seen that the flanges have to be removed to enable it to sit inside the channel.

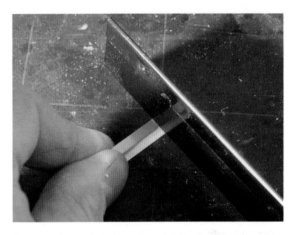

these girders has to be determined. The two baulks were set up using track gauges on the rails to set the distance apart. At least two gauges are required to ensure they are parallel, in order to get an accurate measurement. Sometimes it is easier to have parts made before other parts are made to fit them. The distance measured determines the length of the parts.

Cutting the ends is best done with a hand saw rather than attempting the power saw, as it needs a little more control.

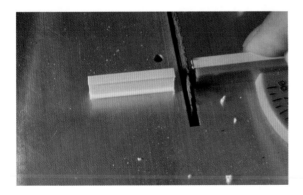

The section cut to 32mm (1.25in). The blade guard has been moved to show the relationship between the guide, the blade and the section – otherwise it is in place when cutting. Even a small saw like this can do considerable damage to fingers.

Having made the saw cuts, the flanges are cut away. A scalpel with a curved blade is the easiest, as it can be rolled into the parts making a progressive cut.

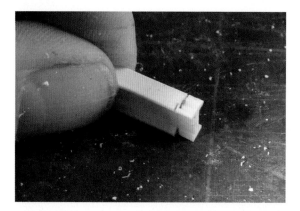

First cut.

The ends are now trimmed to fit inside the channel. At this stage edges need cleaning up. This is done by scraping a scalpel blade along the corners, removing the burrs.

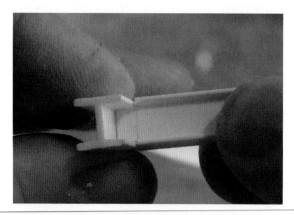

Check the fit. You will note that the 'H'-girder flanges are tapered, so the tongue that fits between needs to be only as wide as the central web.

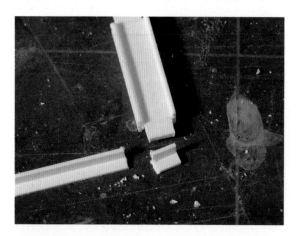

The connecting angle. One is needed each side of the joint on every cross-member. It is cut to the width of web of the girder.

Track spacers fitted, including the corner angles. Situations like this can be a little fiddly as you end up working in a confined area. The cross-piece was fitted first and glued. The angle pieces are dropped on to the girder and pushed into the corner and glued. Gravity can be help to locate the angles; the assembly was held with the cross-piece horizontal and dropping the angle on to it before sliding it into position.

As with other parts, the girder is marked out and cut with a saw. The ends need further work to make them nest inside the flanges of the longitudinal girders. The top and bottom flanges are removed to leave a tongue that fits inside the channel. To complete the assembly of these parts they need small connecting angles that will fit between the tongue and the 'H'-girder web.

When making the model, these were late additions – I forgot! So they were fitted when the bridge was virtually complete. They were slotted into the longitudinal girders spaced between every other cross-girder.

MODIFYING THE TRUSSES

It was at this stage it became apparent that the truss mouldings were a little skinny relative to the other components of the bridge. This could be tackled in two ways: to add material to the vertical sections and to increase the width of the outside flange, or just increase the flange width. I elected for the latter solution as the former would need a lot of butt-jointed components; these would be narrow strips

added between the moulded gusset plates requiring a high degree of accuracy of length and position. Adding just the flange provides a satisfactory visual enlargement of the structure.

ASSEMBLING THE STRUCTURE

Before the final assembly could be started, the longer main cross-members needed to be trimmed to accept the diagonal stays. These and the other cross-members also required the position of the longitudinal member marked to assist location during assembly.

The trusses were used as the basic guide to set up the assembly. First, the rails on their members were set up using the track gauges again to set the distance apart. These rested on the outer cross-members of the first truss. Then, using a rule and square, they were set up in a position that matched the ends of the truss. Once happy with the location, they were bonded to the longitudinal members.

The remaining cross-members were similarly fitted, matching them to the verticals of the truss.

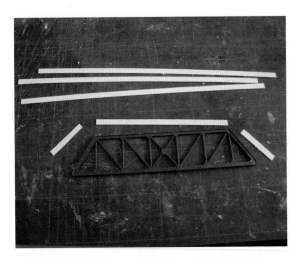

The flange strip cut from 0.040in plasticard; prepared lengths and cut ready to stick. The lengths were taken directly from the moulded truss. It was laid over the strip as a guide and a straight-bladed scalpel aligned and chopped through the strip. It was then stuck to all four sides keeping the truss central.

The girders marked out and the first one trimmed for the diagonal stay. The flange is removed back to the central web. The web provides the location for the stay.

The basic setting-out of the first parts. The square is an essential tool in these circumstances. Note that two types of track gauge are being used. Either type can be used in these situations, as they are setting straight track. Once the track members are stuck to the cross-members, they are no longer needed.

Using a square and rule to set the end member centrally. As the blade of the square is not in contact with the longitudinal member, one has to be carefully 'sighted' against the other to confirm alignment. Note the chairs for the sleepers already in place ready for the sleepers.

Repeating the operation at the other end of the first truss.

RIGHT: Fitting the short cross-members; rule and square to the fore. The middle ones are aligned with the trusses by eye.

The longer cross-members added. Note the cut-outs for the side stays face inwards from each end.

Nearly all the members are in place. The small ones between the longitudinal girders have yet to be fitted. With an assembly like this it is best to check the bond of each component at this stage. Hold it firmly and try and flex each part relative to another. If well bonded it will almost ping, if not add some more adhesive at the troublesome joint ensuring the parts are in contact. A clamp may assist.

ASSEMBLING THE TRUSSES

The next step is to fix the trusses to the base girders and track. The modified trusses are simply lined up with the outer edges of the short cross-girders and adhesive applied. They are checked to ensure they are vertical and in line.

Once the trusses are set in position, the side stays can be added. These are in 'L'-section and fit under the top member of the truss down to the bottom edge of the extended cross-girders. The length of the stays was measured from the assembly.

The section is cut to the measured length: one for every extended girder. They are fixed on the web of the lower girder and along the edge where it touches the truss. It is clear that such a joint is not a good engineering solution and requires some additional fixing – a gusset plate is needed.

A trial gusset was cut out in 0.040in plasticard and offered up to see how it fitted. This checks the overall size and geometry. Once a prototype has been proved, then the remainder can be cut out and attached.

Three out of the four trusses fixed. Now it begins to look like a bridge.

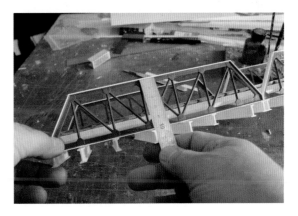

Measuring the length of the side stays. The rule is tucked under the top flange of the truss and the measurement is taken to the corner of between the web and flange of the bottom girder.

*LEFT: **The first of the side stays attached. The small area of contact at the top of the stay is very apparent, especially compared to the area at the bottom.***

The gussets added. This shows a more convincing attachment for the stay. A detail of a gusset, note the relief for the moulded gusset on the truss.

FINAL DETAILS

Once the stays and gussets are in place, the bridge is virtually complete. However, I thought that some final details were needed; these are representations of the rivets fixing the stays and adding some plate work on the corners of the added flange on the truss.

As the parts that form the stay assembly are quite thick, notably the girder and angle, it is not possible to emboss the rivets, even if it were possible to access the parts once assembled.

I made stick-on rivets by embossing some 0.040in plasticard, then shaving off the dimple produced to stick on the parts. A new scalpel blade is essential for successful shaving. The dimple is picked up on the point of the blade and transferred to its location. Adhesive is added to the surface before positioning the dimple. It can be pushed around initially to achieve its correct position.

An alternative to shaving embossed rivets is to chop some from 1mm square or round plastic section. Again they are picked up on the tip of the blade and located on the surface. The difficulty with chopping them is to get consistent short lengths.

The final details are the corner capping angles, which are made from 0.030in plasticard. They were sized to be twice as long as the width of the capping strips. The midpoint was marked, then the part was held in parallel-jawed pliers with midpoint on the

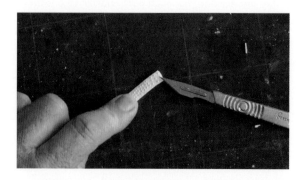

A left-over strip of 0.040in plasticard with multiple embossed rivets to be shaved off. To shave them the blade is placed flat on the surface next to the dimple and slices through on the base surface.

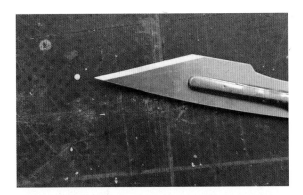

A rivet dimple at the tip of the blade. It helps when working with such tiny parts that you have a contrasting background like the cutting mat to help them show up. Nevertheless, expect to lose a few.

Rivets applied at the bottom of the stay; on the angle and the girder.

Rivets at the top of the stays. Both sides can be seen between the adjacent stays.

A corner cap bent ready for installation. The bend has to be made more than the finished angle, as the plasticard will spring back.

end of the jaws. A bend was made pushing the part through nearly 90 degrees. The part was then stuck over the corner and completed with more stick-on rivet heads.

This completes the construction of the bridge structure. It now remains to make the abutments and the mid-stream pier.

RIGHT: Corner cap in place with rivet heads added. This effectively hides a joint between the capping strip on the top and side.

THE ABUTMENTS AND MIDSTREAM PIER

Once again a sketch was made to determine the sizes of the abutments. I had no prototype information for this bridge so details from other bridges have been adapted to suit. All the parts in the river have notional streamlining to avoid restricting the flow and to deflect any floating debris, so the abutments and central pier reflect this.

One of the abutments. This has been sawn from 0.080in plasticard: one width to make the height and another for the top and bottom surfaces and the spacers. The corners have yet to be rounded with a file.

Marking the upper limit of the brickwork. This has been determined from counting off an appropriate number of bricks on the embossed sheet. It is easier to mark the shorter dimension than the longer if taking the dividers along an edge as a datum. As before, it helps if some pencil lead is rubbed into the line to help it show up.

To this end, two boxes were made from 0.080in plasticard as the end abutments. The corners between the faces are rounded with a file. A line was scribed below the top edge as a guide for the upper edge of the brickwork that abuts the capping stones. The brick finish is embossed plasticard. I have used English Bond finish as this is appropriate to the period modelled and is also typical of the bond used in such structures. (The brick bond is the pattern in which bricks are laid: along the wall 'stretchers', into the wall 'headers'.)

A strip of brick plasticard was cut with a line of headers to go along the top. This was stuck to the base by flooding the surface of the plastic with adhesive and creating a sticky surface. The same was done on the back of the brick. This creates a surface that responds like contact adhesive. The brick is pressed on to the base from the centre of the abutment and folded around the corners. A little extra adhesive may be required, as the solvent dries rapidly. Note, too much adhesive trapped under the brick can soften and distort the brick. The final attachment is especially helped with a little extra adhesive and pressing the surface down to push the brick on to the surface.

A strip of brickwork cut for surfacing the abutment. It is easier if the strip is cut longer than the length of the wall. It stops the embarrassment of not making it long enough, but essentially it can be cut to the exact finished size by trimming the excess. The surface is flooded with solvent, which is brushed around until a sticky surface is achieved. The brick plasticard is similarly treated. The two sticky surfaces bond quickly. Note my bottle holding the adhesive. It is wedged into an MDF base that supports it and prevents it from being knocked over.

After the main face has been stuck, the brick is bent around on to the next sticky surface.

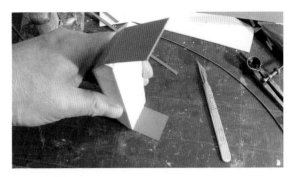

As the ends have the least area for a bond they do not stick so readily as the other surfaces. To help bond this, press the brick on to a surface. Once the brick has been stuck, the excess can be trimmed off.

The profile of the retaining wall has been cut out of 0.080in plasticard and the brick stuck to it. The brick has been trimmed to the profile leaving sufficient to be bent around the ends. If the inner part under the brick plasticard is any thinner than 0.080in, then there is a considerable likelihood of the two parts warping as the adhesive dries.

The assemblies were set aside whilst the adhesive dried. The abutment seats against a retaining wall. This was cut out from 0.080in plasticard and again faced with brick plasticard. The brick has to be folded around the ends, as this is a sharp corner unlike the earlier radiused ones. To make this easier, use the point of the scalpel blade to scribe the inside edge and use the edge of the thicker plasticard to guide it. Keep checking the embossed surface until you can see a pale line of the scribed line, this will be sufficient to make a sharp bend.

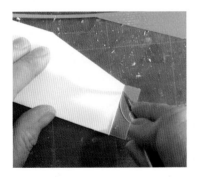

Bend the end around the edge of the base by again scribing the inside with the point of a scalpel. Use the edge of the base material to guide the blade. Check the embossed surface for a register of the scribed line. It should just show like this. Once the line shows it can be bent around the end. Apply adhesive to both the base material and the brick before bending. As the surfaces become sticky push the brick around the corner and press down on the end to force the parts together. Trim the excess when dry.

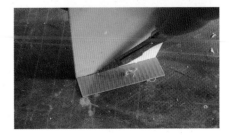

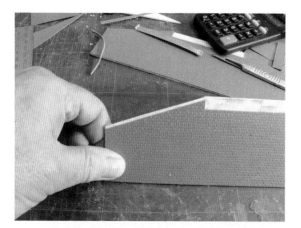

The embossed brick has been cut away for fitting the cap stones. Residual brick plasticard remains on the surface seen by a register of the brick colour. This is of no consequence and will be covered when the cap stones are stuck on.

Apply adhesive to both the base and brick, and immediately fold the brick around the corner, pressing it down as it dries. Once dry, trim the excess brick flush to the base material.

Capping stones are needed on the retaining wall: light ones on the slopes and heavier ones under the track. As the brick currently covers the entire wall, it needs to be trimmed to fit the stones. The brick plasticard is cut through where the capping stones are to be fitted and peeled off. This is obviously best

A strip two bricks deep has been cut out to add relief. In spite of a guide of an embossed line it is still best to use a straight edge along the line to guide the cut.

done before the adhesive completely dries and has to be done with care, as the scalpel blade has to be introduced under the brick to lift it.

Before fitting the capping stones, a second strip of brick was added to the top of the brick on the abutments to generate extra relief. This is stuck from the centre toward the end, bending it around the corners. A clamp helps hold the ends whilst the adhesive dries.

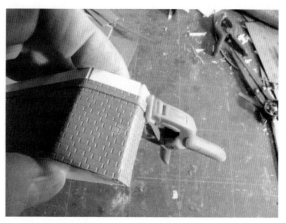

The strip stuck down and bent around the ends. A spring clamp holds the end until it is stuck. Note that the brick pattern on the strip has been matched to the base brick.

The capping stones were cut from a strip of 0.080in plasticard and the long edge was bevelled with a file. The strip was held along the edge of the workbench allowing the file to be held at around 45 degrees to shape the edge. The strip was chopped into lengths that fitted in multiple the length of the wall. The ends of each were filed to produce a chamfer. The individual parts were then stuck in place. Once dry the saw was run between each stone to enhance the mortar line between each and to carry it back into the base material.

The capping on the sloping tops of the retaining wall was treated slightly differently. A strip was fixed into the rebate created in the brickwork, this was then divided into even lengths and the saw used to make the mortar lines.

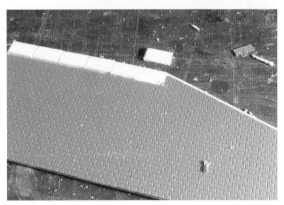

A strip of 0.080in plasticard has been cut for the capping stones. By aligning it with the edge of the worktop, a file can be used to bevel the edge. This strip is then cut into individual stones. The ends are again bevelled with a file. The individual stones are then stuck into the recess made to receive them. Fitting them individually introduces a slight unevenness that makes the appearance less clinical.

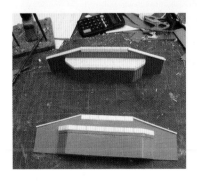

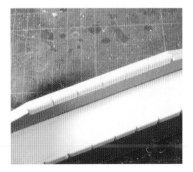

The larger capping stones on the top of the retaining wall have been fitted. The mortar joints between the stones are cut into the edge to complete the appearance. The retaining wall capping is similarly treated. In this instance the smaller section strip is divided after fixing; easier than a number of small items in this case.

The central pier was made in a similar way to the abutments, except is an enclosed box. Again, 0.080in plasticard is the foundation, cut into strips. The sides, base and top are supported by pieces of 0.080in plasticard cut from earlier off-cuts; two edges with a 90-degree corner were needed for this. A pair were made and then joined to complete the box. The cutwater ends were added from separate pieces to form a V. Once the adhesive was dry, the corners were rounded with a file.

Fitting the brick plasticard. Again there is an allowance for fitting capping stones. The start of the brick is nominally half-way along the pier. This allows a good attachment before it is bent around the shape. Each surface is glued and the brick pressed on to it. Where the brick goes around the tight end corner you can just make out the brick lifting slightly before the bend. In this case add a little more adhesive and press it down. Continue the brick around until nominally half-way down the other side.

The completed box has had the ends added to make the cutwater. At the point a strip of plasticard has been added to reinforce and increase the area that is bonded. The ends have been filed round.

Brick plasticard was again added. Two strips were cut and the first was attached from about half-way down one side. This was then wrapped and glued around the ends until it was about half-way down the other side. Care has to be taken that the bottom edge remains coincident with the bottom edge of the base structure; any unevenness in the rounded corner can deflect the sheet off the path it needs to take.

The second brick sheet was butted up to the first. Make sure the brick pattern is maintained, with no uneven lengths of brick. You will find that the adhesive will melt the brick plasticard to a degree, causing it to flow out of the joint. With care this can be used to help blur the joint. This sheet is wrapped around the other end and will overlap the first. Do not glue the overlap. Using a square, cut through both sheets simultaneously following a vertical mortar line. The

A second sheet of brick is cut to complete the other end. The embossed bricks have been cut so that the courses match the headers and stretchers. If the join shows as this in the middle, add some adhesive to soften the joint and with a finger nail rub the surface to blur the line. Once dry the mortar lines can be recovered with a scriber.

The second piece of brick plasticard is wrapped until it overlaps the first. It is cut following the vertical mortar courses, the cut continuing into the first layer. The two cuts are now coincident and have a common edge. The first layer under the second is removed and the second layer glued to abut the first. There is likely to be a mismatch in the courses but this can be hidden by blurring the joint as described earlier.

end of the top sheet can be discarded. The previously fitted brick will now have a cut line down it. Remove the outer portion, lifting it with a scalpel and peeling it off. The second sheet can now be glued to the base with a perfect abutment to the first brick sheet.

The capping stones can now be added and finished as were the earlier ones.

This bridge is to be used on a future layout. One of the features of this layout is that it is in an area of red brick. This area produces a brick that is softer than some so exhibits a higher degree of weathering than many. To this end it has been distressed using a burr in the modelling drill, scraping and excavating with a scalpel blade and generally roughened with wet and dry paper.

The capping stones have been added from a strip created as for the abutments. A single thinner triangular has been fitted above the cutwater. Its edges have been filed round. The top surface of the pier has had the mortar lines cut into it and the inner line scribed parallel to edges.

Distressed brickwork. Mortar lines have been deepened, bricks cut out and brick surfaces cut into by the burr. A random approach is needed but certain areas are more likely to be damaged, like the upstream corners. Floating debris, especially at times of flood, will strike and gouge the brickwork at water level and just above. Follow the mortar courses when removing bricks. The tools are illustrated: a wire brush, wet and dry paper, a scalpel with a new blade, and the drill with the burr. The burr used here is about 1.5mm in diameter. Use a smaller one for smaller scale brickwork.

A round burr has been applied to individual bricks; easier in 7mm scale but a smaller burr will work in the smaller scales. Do not set the drill speed too fast otherwise the burr will melt the surface rather than cutting it. The operation is entirely by eye; aim to achieve a random pattern. If your joints in the brick sheets are less than perfect the distress can make them less apparent. The burr has also been used to roughen the surface of the capping stones. Apply lightly and allow it to skip over the surface making small indentations.

Use a scalpel to carve larger or deeper mortar joints. Individual and multiple bricks can be cut out following the mortar lines. Scratch the surface of some bricks with the point of the blade to create further relief. Rub the whole surface with 60 grit (finer for smaller scales) wet and dry to generally roughen the finish. Finally use a brass wire brush to remove any loose pieces created in the earlier operations.

This now completes both bridge and supporting structures. I have not painted this example as it is moving onward to a future installation.

The completed bridge and supports. The bridge and supports have yet to be attached to each other. This will happen after painting and on its final installation.

CHAPTER EIGHT

A MASONRY ARCH BRIDGE

THE PROTOTYPE

The bridge chosen to illustrate construction is built in engineering blue brick. The brick courses are laid in English bond, which is alternate courses of stretchers, bricks laid lengthwise, and headers, bricks laid with short side showing. Walls built in this form have good interlocking structure. The capping stones and stringers are in local stone, which in this case is blue lias. Unlike the brick it does not weather well, the edges are splitting and eroding.

The bridge is also slightly on the skew: the road passing under the tracks is not at 90 degrees to them but closer to 80 degrees. It is possible to measure this in several ways, as photographs rarely do more than indicate the skew. First, if it is a quiet road, a right-angled triangle can be constructed in the roadway using the abutment as the hypotenuse of the triangle and then by trigonometry or measuring to find the angle. Second, the location can be found on an Ordnance Survey map and the angle measured on that. The larger the scale, the more accurate it will be. Third, the aerial view provide by Google Earth can provide the same information as a map.

THE MODEL

A brick structure lends itself to sizing by counting bricks. Take a print of your photographic reference, enlarging if necessary, so it can be written on. This may be less easy from some printed books due to the method of reproduction, where shades of grey are made up in dots; enlarging can lose detail. If this appears to be a problem, then select the clearest number of bricks and set that number on a pair of dividers. Do this both horizontally and vertically. This will not work if the image is deeply oblique, as the foreshortening compresses the distance. However, in a view that is only slightly off-square to the viewer

this can safely be ignored. These multiples can then be stepped along the image to get an overall size.

For this model I am using a laminated form of construction where the basic parts are separated by spacing strips to form hollow sections. The shapes of the main walls are cut out of 0.040in plasticard and spaced with strips from the Plastruct or Evergreen ranges. If you are able to cut consistent widths from 0.040in plasticard sheet, then this can be used as an alternative. The separating strips should not form enclosed spaces, which will retain adhesive vapours – if these cannot escape, then they will continue to work on the structure, softening it. The aim is to get an overall thickness of about $^3/_{16}$in or 5mm, perhaps less. Walls made like this are rigid and do not distort when laminating further layers of plasticard to them;

The picture of the bridge and a representative sheet of English bond embossed plasticard. The bricks have been counted in various features: the height of the buttresses to the string course, the width of the buttresses, the height above the string course, etc. The widths are done in a similar manner. If possible with this bond use the stretchers for this. The bricks are counted out on the plasticard sheet and the numbers measured to provide a dimension. It is handy to annotate these on the picture.

they are relatively lightweight too. This 'cavity wall' can be used in all scales. In the smaller scales I would suggest that the basic sheet thickness should not be less than 0.030in, as thinner material will be subject to greater softening and distortion when laminating the brick or stone finish.

CONSTRUCTION

SETTING OUT THE PARTS

Once you have a set of dimensions, the parts of the bridge can be drawn. The basis for the spandrel face of the bridge is 0.040in thick white plasticard. To draw the bridge, select one edge of the plasticard as a datum and put it to the bottom of the sheet to work from that. Using a set square, check that the left-hand corner is a right angle; if not, either cut the plasticard to make a new edge or draw a line close to the edge square to the datum. This is now your left-hand vertical datum. Mark the line that will be the vertical centreline of the arch. To assist with drawing on the plasticard, lightly roughen the surface with a kitchen scourer, the green one used dry – an HB pencil then shows up.

Complete the vertical and horizontal leading dimensions. Set the height for the lower edge of the

The compass cutter in use. The cutting edge is lined up with the outside edge of the line drawn. The cutting edge is drawn around the arc several times, deepening the groove. The groove it cuts is nominally the same width as the thickness of the plasticard. Note that a commercial compass cutter can be used rather than a modified draughting compass.

arch each side, then set the height of the arch on the centreline. The arch is drawn by trial and error. Place the compass point on the vertical centreline somewhere near the bottom; set the compass lead on to the mark for the lowest point of the arch and swing the compass to see if the arc the lead traces

Using a beam compass to draw the arch. An ordinary compass will do just as well. What are not shown are the multiple indentations of the trial compass points. The general outline of the bridge face can be seen. This is now ready to be cut out.

The arch cut away. Cutting the curve has been completed with a scalpel. Two cuts along the inside walls releases the shape. The remainder of the spandrel wall is cut out.

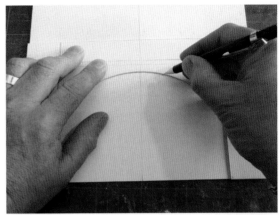

*ABOVE AND RIGHT: **The wall is traced on to the plasticard. Note the centreline drawn on the profile matched to a line drawn on the sheet. The copied parts are cut out in the same way as the first. The faces that were against the first profile have been marked as 'Inside'. These will be assembled facing the original and one of its copies.***

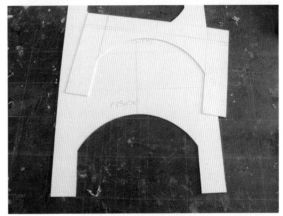

passes through the highest point of the arch. It is unlikely you will be right first time.

If the pencil lead passes above the top of the arch, reduce the radius slightly, set the lead on the lowest point of the arch and reset the point on the centreline. Try the arc again. Keep adjusting until the drawn arc passes all three points of the arch. Mark the centre point that works for reference. If the arc passes below the top of the arch, increase the radius slightly; the opposite of that described above. It is trial and error.

Once a satisfactory outline has been achieved the shape can be cut out. Start with the curve of the arch. By far the easiest way of cutting the curve is to use a compass cutter – a commercial one or, as I have, modified draughting compasses. The cut does not have to go completely through the plasticard. The cut can be completed with a scalpel or craft knife once the cut line goes about half-way through. The groove will guide the blade. The two vertical cuts at the end of the arch are made next and then the final outline cuts.

The first one cut out can be used as a template and the profile copied from it for the remaining three sheets. If copying, it is essential that the arch centreline is marked out clearly. This acts as a datum for the subsequent parts.

ASSEMBLING THE SPANDREL FACES

The parts are paired up and any notes to yourself about 'way round' written on them. You may find you wish to relegate a part with some damage, a false cut for instance, to a position where the cut is not visible.

The parts are separated by strips of plastic. I have used Evergreen 0.040 × 0.188in strip in this instance. Similar strips can be cut from a sheet but only if sawn together will they be of consistent width. The same accuracy cannot be achieved using a blade against a straight edge.

The curve of the arch is done first. Take a strip and pull it between finger and thumb, at the same

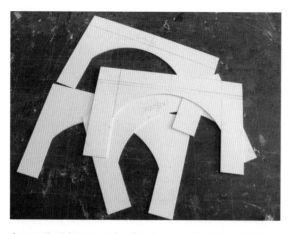 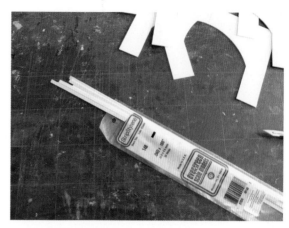

A set of arches and the Evergreen strip that will space them apart; the dimensions of this strip are 0.040 × 0.188in. The thickness of the strip is the same as the thickness of the sheet. It should not be less but can be more.

 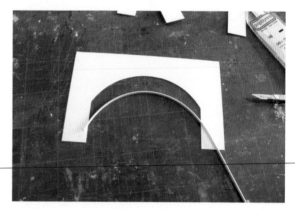

The strip is formed to match the curve of the arch. Pulling it between the fingers and curving it at the same time will create the shape. Do not trim the strip fully until after it has been fitted.

time bending it. This will set the curve in the strip. Match to the length of the arch curve and trim to length. Starting at one end, apply adhesive. Align the strip with the edge of the curve. The corner of a square can be used to push the strip using the arch to limit the movement of the square. Once the arch is in place the two verticals can be added each

Gluing the strip. Start at one end and progress to the other. The strip is sitting on top of the spandrel sheet and the edges are matched as the gluing progresses. There can be a slight tendency for the strip to straighten, but the initial curving limits this.

The strip being added to the vertical edge: a square has been pushed against the edge of the sheet cut-out and the strip pushed against it. Take care with the adhesive: it can spill around the strip and get between the square and strip, trying to bond the strip to the square.

Further strips are added to space the second sheet. A nominal symmetry is advisable but it does not have to be precise. Gaps are left at the ends to allow the eventual enclosed space to ventilate.

A generous coat of adhesive is spread over the surface, making it tacky. The inner wall is added aligning the arch and side walls. Further adhesive is added along the arch, side-wall strips and inside the edges.

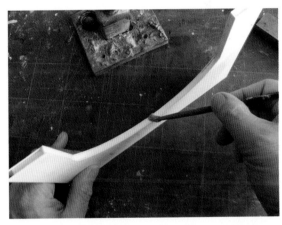

Run further adhesive into the join to ensure a bond.

side. A square can again be used to get the position and ensure the strips are square to the surface. The face then has a further strip added to support the second spandrel face. Unlike the arch parts, these do not have to be against an edge, only square to the surface. Allow the adhesive to dry before adding the second face.

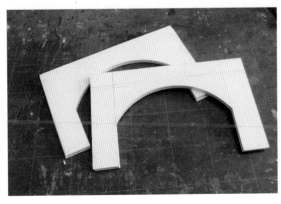

Two complete arch walls.

Once dry, apply a generous application of adhesive across the face of the second spandrel wall. Let the surface become tacky and immediately apply it to the first wall with spacers aligning the arch. Complete the join by applying further adhesive to the arch strip and to the strip visible around the edges. Use a generous application here, especially as it will run into the interior, reinforcing the adhesion of the hidden parts. Repeat for the second wall.

THE DECK

The deck is constructed in a similar way to the walls. The width suits either the road carriageway or the

number of tracks across the span. The lengths need to run beyond the ends of the parapet to blend into the road or rail bed.

Two rectangular sheets are cut to the appropriate size. On one the strips are fitted, two lengths along the long edge – these will provide attachment to the spandrel walls. The remainder are added in a zigzag pattern, which will provide not only the necessary stiffness, but resist any tendency to twist. The second sheet is added after flooding the surface with adhesive to make it tacky, with more around the edges once the parts have come together.

ADDING THE BRICKWORK

The bridge has a string course of stone just above the arch, which defines the upper limit of the brickwork at this stage. The edge of a sheet of embossed brick plasticard is aligned with the bottom edge of the string course, plain side upwards, and the outline of the arch and walls are drawn on to it. This defines the notional area where adhesive will be spread.

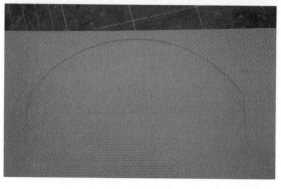

The deck cut to size and spacing strips added. Strips along the edge are important as they provide an area to bond the deck to the walls. The zig-zag pattern minimizes twist in the completed structure.

*OPPOSITE AND ABOVE: **The shape of the wall is outlined on the back of a brick sheet. This defines the area that adhesive will be applied to. The top edge of the brick is aligned with the string course. Adhesive is flooded over the brick and the walls and the two brought together. Once dry the brick is trimmed back to the wall.***

The wall assembly is spread with a generous application of adhesive, again creating a tacky surface, except around the arch, as the brick is cut away later, so a poor bond here is desirable. The same is done to the brick. The two are brought together, aligning the edge with the line of the string course. Press them together and they will stick. If adhesive is applied as they come together there is a danger that some will be trapped in a pocket between the surfaces. Unable to evaporate it will dissolve its way out, usually through the brick!

Once the adhesive has set the arch can be cut out. The edge of the wall will guide the blade.

ADDING THE DECK

This bridge has a small skew, one arch offset relative to the other; the deck needs some reference marks to indicate the amount. If there is no offset, then reference marks still help with alignment.

The deck is fixed to one wall, ensuring it is in its relative position to the wall. The second wall is fixed with the appropriate offset, again ensuring it is at

Once the two sides are in place, the offset of one to the other for the skew is shown by the rule nominally on the arch centreline. Fitting the rule in the corner between the arch and wall shows the contact between outer skin on the left and the inner on the right. This needs to be straightened for the fit of the inner wall. The square initially shows the amount to be removed on the inner skin for this straightening and the subsequent gap after removing the material.

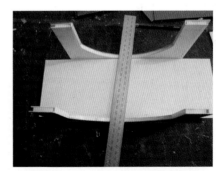
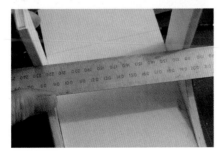

right angles to the deck. Allow the adhesive to dry before moving on, as the assembly of these parts is not as strong as the final assembly confers.

The first side is attached to the deck – note the pencil mark to align the first part. From this the offset of the skew is marked and the second side is added. The rule is nominally sitting on the centreline of the arch. If a straight edge is placed in the corner where the arch meets the side wall, it can be seen that at one end the edge is on the outside wall and at the other on the inside wall. In order to make a straight wall connecting the arches, the inside wall needs to be trimmed back – the amount can be judged by eye. A guideline is drawn set back the appropriate amount from the edge and the material shaved away to the line.

FILLING THE ARCH

Measure the distance between the inside walls. Do this against the deck to avoid an incorrect measurement by flexing the walls. Cut a rectangle of 0.040in plasticard to the measured length by the height of the vertical wall and glue in position. Repeat for the other side.

This wall is somewhat flexible, so needs stiffening. Cut strips of the same thickness material to slightly

shorter than the nominal length of the wall. The number needed will depend on the height of the wall – this assembly has three. The ends need to be joined to the walls. Cut squares nominally the same size as the width of the strips and glue to the surface of the strip and to the end walls. The parts are now linked.

The curved surface of the arch can now be made using thinner plasticard, 0.020 or 0.030in, two layers laminated together. Initially, roll the plasticard up, as tight a roll as you can get – this will pre-form it to the curve. Press the sheet on to the arch forms. Fit an edge to the end of the arch at the wall junction; press the sheet around until it sits in the opposite corner and mark this point. This now shows the length of the arc and the point at which to cut off the excess.

An alternative to this is to take a thin strip of plasticard and form around the curve, one end in the corner and cut it off where it meets the other corner. This also gives the length of the arc. Transfer the dimension to the sheet and trim to suit.

Glue the sheet on to the arches. Start at one end, rolling it down as adhesive is applied each side. With that in place, add the second layer.

As this is a skew arch bridge, the brickwork has a special alignment. At the apex of the arch the bricks are square to the arch faces with mortar lines running

The wall panel is fitted between the walls after measuring to determine its size. Strips of 0.040in plasticard are stuck behind to stiffen the wall. As the ends are not at 90 degrees to the walls these are slightly shorter than the length of the panel. Small squares are glued at each end making up the difference and connecting squarely to the walls.

 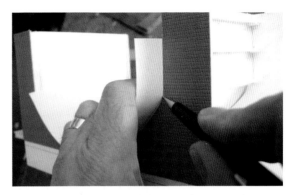

A sheet of 0.030in plasticard is pressed into the arch space. One edge is aligned with the corner between the arch and the wall. Holding it firmly in place, the opposite corner is marked.

This shows the alternative method of measuring the length of the arc. A strip of plasticard is pressed around the curve and cut to length. This length can then be transferred to the plasticard sheet.

Rolling the plasticard sheet like this encourages it to hold its curve whilst being stuck in position. It is only possible with the thinner sheets.

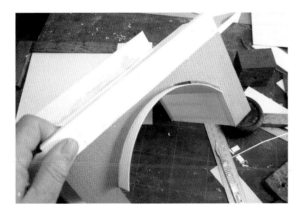 

Gluing the trimmed arch in place. Start adding adhesive at one end and press the sheet into place. The sheet is longer than the width of the bridge – this is trimmed later. The second sheet follows and its length is determined in the same way as the first. Be sparing with adhesive joining the two layers and do not trap it in a pocket between them.

parallel to the arch axis. For guidance, highlight the horizontal mortar lines on the embossed brick; an HB pencil does nicely. Do this on the sheet nominally where the top of the arch will come. Line up the marked line with the arch axis and then, pressing the sheet on to the earlier formed arch, mark the intersection with the vertical walls. Draw a line before cutting to these marks. This line will cut across the bricks at an angle; in this case a shallow angle, as the skew is small, but at a greater angle if the skew is more pronounced. Cut a little oversize initially to be sure of the fit. Trim when happy.

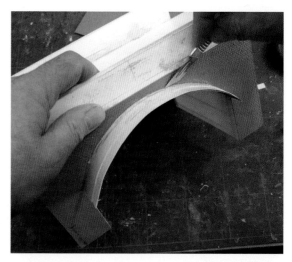

Trim the three layers of the arch flush with the spandrel wall face. Take a series of cuts, do not try to do it in one go. The pressure of the cut can undo the joint, worse the blade can break damaging you or the model.

The brick sheet has a pencil mark to help align the courses square to the spandrel walls. Hold, keeping the alignment mark true and trim the sheet to match the plain ones. Glue the trimmed brick into position.

Glue the brick sheet into place in the same manner as the plain sheets. Once the brick is secure, the three sheets forming the arch can be trimmed back to the faces of the arch. Draw the knife around in a series of cuts. Do not try to do it in one go; it is almost certain to go awry.

This shows the trimmed sheet meeting the wall at an angle, due to the skew of the bridge.

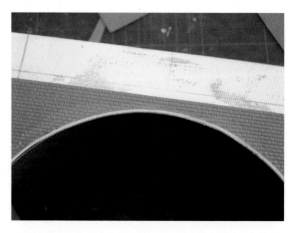

The finished end may show that one or more layers have not been stuck, as the left-hand side of the arch illustrates. Adding a little adhesive and pressing the gap closed should remedy the situation.

MAKING THE ARCH RINGS

The arch rings are the bricks that appear at the end of an arch. These are the bricks that have been laid on the formwork making the arch during construction. For a stone bridge the arch rings will be in stone, where they will have an apparent keystone at the top or they may appear as voussoirs.

This bridge has three rows flush and a fourth decorative projecting row. The three rows need to be inset; the fourth can be added on top. To make the space for the rows, the dividers are set to three rows taken from the embossed brick sheet. The point is then run around the arch, scribing a line inset from the arch. The scribed line is then cut through the earlier applied brickwork. A blade is carefully inserted between the brick and base plasticard, lifting the brick away. It is now apparent why minimal adhesive is needed in this area – the plasticard forming the arches needs to be trimmed back to the new surface.

The brickwork of this bridge is English bond: successive headers and stretchers. Cut out a line of headers (the short brick ends) and at the same time, cut out rows of stretchers but do not discard them as they will be used later. Take the strip of headers and form to a curve on a flat surface; push it around with your fingers. Take this strip and glue it to the curve of the arch. Start at one end on the outside following the edge of the arch. Glue it in stages, checking its position all the time. Trim to length when you reach the other end. Add the second row following the first. Do not worry if the mortar courses are not staggered, in this situation they often are not. Finally, add the third. These should now fill the area cut away.

Marking out for the arch rings. The dividers have been set to three brick-courses wide. One point follows the curve; the second scribes the line to be cut. Deepen the scribed line with a scalpel blade cutting through the embossed brick. Remove the brick between the arch and line by shaving with the blade. This is easier if the brick has not been well stuck, as suggested. The three layers of the arch need to be shaved back to the base plasticard. The space is now ready to have the arch rings inserted.

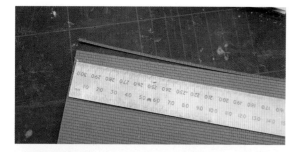

The arch courses are made from header courses. Cut these as strips from the embossed plasticard. Four of these strips are needed. Do not discard the stretcher strips that are in between. Bend the strips in the flat before sticking them in place. The first ring is stuck next to the arch, ensuring it abuts the edge. Follow up with the second and third strips. The mortar course will not stagger as in a normal brick course. Try to avoid gaps between the strips.

The decorative row can now be added following the curve – the stretcher strips can be used for this, formed to a curve as were the other strips. The first strip is stuck in place next to the edge of the cutaway area, a second strip is stuck to that and a third of headers added on top of that to complete the decorative row. On the prototype this row has a distinctive round edge. This can be added by scraping off the corners when the adhesive is well and truly set. When gluing thin sections like this, the plastic remains softened by the adhesive for some time, so can be disturbed.

Take the stretcher course strips and add them on the surface next to the last header strip. Bend it as the other strips. Take the second strip and add it on top of the first to create the basis of the decorative arch ring. Complete it with the fourth header strip. When the adhesive is dry and the strips are secure the corners can be scraped to round off the section.

Scraping the edge of the buttress plasticard to produce the radius on the edge. It could be filed but there is a fair chance that the middle will have the most complete radius and the ends lesser radii. Try the shaped part to check it has not become undersize.

ADDING THE BUTTRESSES

The buttresses on this bridge are quite thin compared to some. They also feature a radiused edge by the arch. A single thickness of 0.080in plasticard is a suitable basis for them. The parts were cut to fit the width beside the arch and between the ground line and the string course. One edge was radiused

by scraping with the edge of a scalpel blade – this is more effective than using a file. The blade is held nominally at 90 degrees and is drawn along the edge, peeling away the plastic. This is also less messy than filing, which generates a static charge on the plastic causing it to stick on everything.

The brick plasticard is stuck to the foundation

Stick the brick plasticard to the base material allowing a generous overlap at the edge with the radius. Once the adhesive is dry, the brick can be folded around the radius. Flood the parts with adhesive and press down hard, pushing the brick around the corner; take it well beyond 90 degrees, attempt to take it around the second corner too. There will be a degree of spring back in the brick, so clamping it may help hold, though this is difficult on a thin section like this. If the wall was deeper, then there is a larger surface around the corner to help hold the brick once forced around the corner. This would be easier to clamp, if needed.

The excess brick is cut away using the edges of the base as a guide. The buttress is then glued in place. The brick that goes around the corner should be proud of the inner vertical wall surface.

The gap between the buttresses and the edge of the arch is measured and a brick rectangle is cut to fit. In situations like this it is usually easier to make a part to fit than to make something in advance hoping it will fit.

part in the same way as earlier applications, flooding the surface to make it sticky and pressing the pieces together. Note the arrangement of the brick courses on the arch face; for example, if at ground level, they are stretchers, so stretchers at the bottom of the buttress. Allow sufficient brick for trimming.

The brick has to go around the radius previously created. Once the brick is attached to the surface it can be turned around the corner. A little bit of force is needed for this particular application. The brick is folded around the corner through significantly more than 90 degrees. Press the edge down on a surface, trapping the brick, and rotate the part around the edge, forcing the brick around the radius. Once the fold is established, add generous amount of glue and press the parts together. Hold until the glue grabs. Clamping can assist but is difficult on a thin part.

If this were a thicker buttress, the area beyond the radius would make it easier to stick the brick, as there would be a greater area to attach to. Trim the brick to the edges of the base, using the edges to guide the blade. The trimmed buttress can now be stuck to the face of the arch.

With the buttresses in place the brick face can be added to the wall inside the arch. Measure the edge-to-edge dimensions of the surface to be covered and cut the brick to fit.

THE STRING COURSE

The string course of the bridge is in local stone, blue lias; its quarried form allows thin slabs to be cut. It is also used for the capping of all the walls. The courses are strips cut from 0.080in plasticard nominally 0.080 wide. If sawn there is a chance that the strip can rotate against the blade and have a rough bevelled edge cut across the edge. This can be used as a weathering feature where the edges of the stones break off. The strips are cut to nominal scale 3ft (0.9m) lengths. The strips are then stuck above the brickwork in two rows. End joints are staggered as in brick courses.

THE PARAPET

The brickwork for this is added above the string courses. A further layer of brick is added to the inside above the decking and on this are the pilasters above the buttresses. If a length of 0.080in plasticard, totalling the length of all eight additions, is prepared, then a single part can be covered in brick and then subsequently cut to length to make the pilaster additions. A small piece of embossed brick is stuck on the

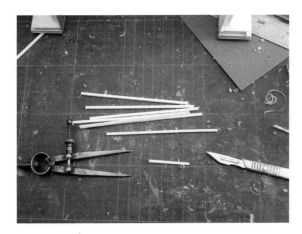

The string course is cut from 0.080in plastic to a nominally square section. Cutting thin strips like this with a saw can leave an edge that is not square; the rotation of the blade drags the strip around slightly. In this instance it is not a problem as the edge can be used for the weathering effect on the stone. The strips are cut to nominal scale 2 or 3ft lengths and stuck in place above the top edge of the brick. Two layers are built up for this bridge but other bridges could have a single thickness or more than two string courses. It could be in brick rather than stone too. The brick to the top of the parapet is added once the string courses are in place.

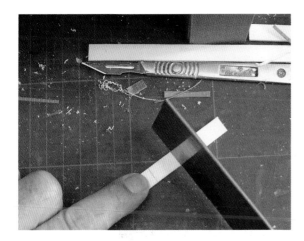

The coping stone strip having the dividing mortar courses added. The strip is divided into suitable scale lengths of the individual stones. The dimensions can be walked off with a pair of dividers. At each mark a saw cut is made partially into the surface and into the edges.

ends to complete the end. Trim once the adhesive is dry.

The parapet and pilasters need coping and cap stones. In common with the string courses, the coping stones are cut from 0.080in plasticard. A strip wide enough to provide a small overhang is cut and divided up into 'stones' about scale 3ft (0.9m) long. The division between the stones is enhanced by a saw cut, which needs to go completely through the thickness at each edge. To represent weathering effects, the corners along the edge are removed in a random fashion, simply sliced off. The joints are deepened in a similar way. The strip is then attached along the top between the pilasters.

The cap stone is made from the same thickness plasticard built up as a stepped pyramid in three layers. The steps are removed by filling with appropriate filler. For plastics there is either Revell

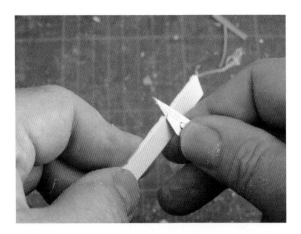

The edges of the strip are cut randomly to represent the weathering of the stone on this bridge. The edges at the joints need some extra emphasis. A V cut into the joint serves to do this. It can be deep or shallow depending how much weathering you wish to represent. On other bridges with harder stone that resists weathering this will not be necessary.

The coping stone has been added to the parapet. The first and second layers of the pilaster cap have been added; the third will follow, building up a stepped pyramid. The first has had its edges worked. This not necessary for the subsequent ones as they are covered in filler and filed to shape.

The filler has been applied over the cap. The rough appearance results from the application of a finger to the surface, pressing it into place. Once dry it is filed to shape. In doing this both filler and plastic are shaped.

'Plasto' or Squadron Putty, green or white (there is no apparent difference between the colours). Epoxy putty like Milliput, fine white, is an alternative. Once hardened it is filed to shape. It is easier to do this *in situ* rather than making the cap stones as separate items to be attached later.

The plastic filler can be smeared across the surface of the coping stones to enhance the texture. A rough surface can be produced by dabbing a finger on the surface whilst it is still tacky or it can be mechanically abraded once hardened. Coarse wet and dry or a burr in the modelling drill can be used to great effect.

THE WING WALLS

The wing walls are constructed in the same way as the spandrel wall: two layers spaced apart. The dimensions of the wall are taken and it is drawn on to 0.040in plasticard.

The shape drawn is not the final shape. Draw it with right-angle corners to start with. These will be modified when fitting the part to the bridge. Offering up the part to the bridge shows that it only fits with the wall square to the spandrel face. The wall can be leant back to represent the batter but the splay cannot be accommodated. The angle in two dimen-

sions results in the bottom edge moving clear of the base of the bridge. To obtain the fit, material equal to the gap has to be removed from the top of the wall. With this removed the wall will now site against the spandrel wall of the arch. The final correction is to return the lower end vertical. With the bridge on a flat surface, hold the wall in place and offer up a square to the end and mark a vertical line; it is then trimmed to the revised shape.

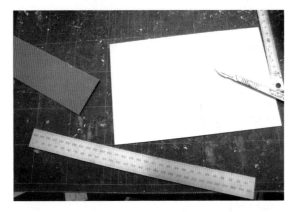

Marking out and cutting the pattern for the wing wall. At this stage it only fits parallel to the roadway. The adjustment for the splay has not yet been made.

Measuring the height of the wing wall. The slope or batter has been matched against the prototype photo.

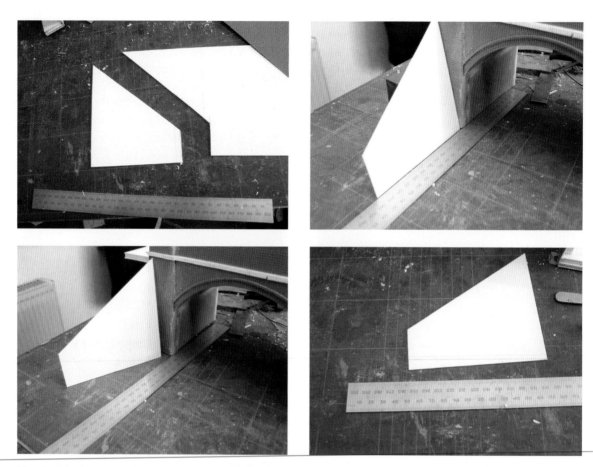

Try the blank against the abutment. It fits with batter (leaning back), but when splayed, a gap on the vertical edge opens up. The gap is measured and the amount is removed from the bottom edge. The gap dimension is measured at the narrow end and diminishes toward the other. The line drawn shows this. It will vary depending on the angle of splay.

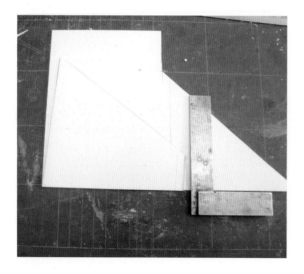

The wall can now be duplicated to make a further seven. Trace it on to a 0.040in plasticard, nesting the shapes together to minimize waste. The parts can then be cut out.

Once the new base line for the compound angle of batter and splay is established, the end for the newel needs correcting. This is cut parallel to the edge that fits against the abutment. The new line shows beside the set square.

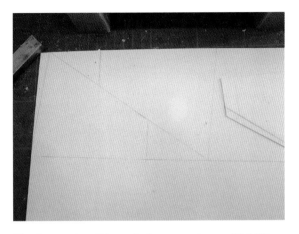

The 'master' wall is copied on to a sheet of 0.040in plasticard. Note how the sloping tops can be nested one against another.

A set of walls waiting assembly.

Four of the shapes are designated as the parts that will eventually have the brick surface – mark the outside to show this. On the other surface, the spacing strips are added and are stuck away from the edges. Their position is not important; just ensure they are square to the surface.

Offer one wall up to the bridge with slopes, batter and splay. It may help to temporarily tape it in position. The inner wall can then be positioned in its relevant place. You will note that it is displaced slightly relative to the outer wall. Add adhesive to join them together. Repeat for the other three wing walls.

Attach the brick to the outer faces. Match the brick course at the bottom to the lower course of the spandrel wall. This course follows the bottom edge of the wing wall. Trim the brick to the profile of the wall.

The inner wall added. Note the displacement of inner to outer that leaves the ends parallel to the bridge face; see the edge of the rule, providing a location for the newel post.

The wall assemblies laid out on a sheet of brick plasticard. It is worth checking with multiple items that are to be further laminated whether or not a number or all can be done on one sheet. Each assembly has been marked with reference to its intended position, left or right. Do this on the inside face. It is easy to apply the laminate on the wrong face without marking.

The wall offered up to the buttress; there is slight gap on the brick face that can be removed by scraping the corner to produce a sharp edge on the brick, which will allow it to sit tightly against the abutment. There is a larger gap behind, which can be filled with a strip stuck to the surface of the wall with its edge on the abutment.

The walls can now be fixed to the buttresses. Now that brick has been attached there will be a small gap at the joint. Scrape or file a chamfer into the base sheet behind the brick to create a sharp edge where the brick meets brick – this is the essential part of

The four sides of the newel post have been cut out and a long and short side glued together. This makes an 'L' shape. A pair of sides is joined together completing the box. A small structure like this does not need the double-wall assembly of the large ones made previously. The bottom end is closed with a further rectangle of plasticard to support the shape.

the joint. The back sheet may not now contact the buttress. This can be addressed by adding a strip to fill the gap when gluing the wall in place.

THE NEWEL AND COPING STONES

The wing walls are completed with addition of the newel at their ends and the copings stones down the slope of the walls.

The newel is made as a box in 0.040in plasticard: the sides and ends are cut out and initially joined on one side and one end to form an 'L' shape. Once the adhesive is dry, join two sets together to make a box.

Cover the box with brick plasticard. The brick only needs to go around three sides of the newel. The fourth side is lost in the soil of the embankment – though there may be exceptions to this. Stick the brick to the longest side of the newel. When dry, use the point of a scalpel to score along the inside of the corner, thinning the brick plasticard to make a hinge. Add adhesive and fold around on to the short sides. When dry trim the brick.

The newels can then be fixed to the wing walls. A cap stone is made in the same manner as the cap on the pilasters. Similarly, coping stones are made as before to fit the tops of the wing walls.

This completes construction of the bridge. It now awaits installation.

The newel structures have been stuck to a strip of brick plasticard in pairs, making a production line of the assembly. The pairs are separated between structures and the brick scored from behind to make a fold around the corners. The score can just be made out on the embossed surface. Glue is added and the sides bent around and then trimmed.

ABOVE MIDDLE: **The newel in place with a bare cap stone and coping stones on the wing wall. The cap is completed with some filler applied in the same way as the pilaster to complete the shape and add further texture.**

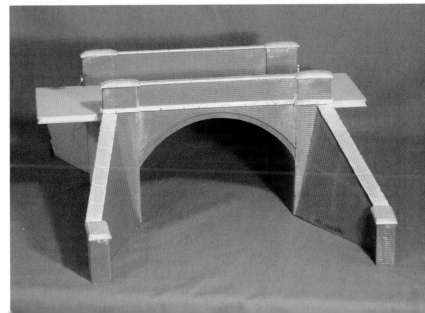

RIGHT: **The completed bridge awaiting colouring and installation.**

CHAPTER NINE

A PLATE-GIRDER BRIDGE

THE PROTOTYPE

I have chosen in this instance to create a generic structure to illustrate various detail features. The span and height have been derived from the table on page 84 for a single-line bridge over a secondary road.

Using prototype pictures, the depth of the main web plate should be around 6ft (1.8m). The web plate is divided into near square sections by vertical stiffeners. These constrain the buckling of the web under load. Allowing that the girder needs to seat on the abutment, then the edge of the abutment coincides with the first of these stiffeners. A seat can be of variable length but 3ft (0.9m) seemed to be right. The web is then divided between these two positions; in this case into five panels.

Flanges are fitted around the web plate to further stiffen it. As the bridge bends under load, the top flange is compressed. If this is too thin it will be unstable and buckle; therefore, it generally has additional layers of platework, in reducing lengths, to increase the thickness of the top flange towards the centre. The bottom flange is under tension when loaded and is stable, requiring only enough additional layers to carry the tensile load.

The bridge components, whether wrought iron in early structures or the more common steel in later bridges, are assembled by riveting. The rivet heads and tails are prominent features. Modern bridges are often welded but will still exhibit the same features of doubling and stiffening though they will lack the attachment flanges needed for a riveted structure. Weld beads will be obvious along components but I would suggest they are too small to consider incorporating in a model.

THE MODEL

Using the derived dimensions, the girder was initially drawn to scale, which enabled me to work out the spacing of the stiffening webs and the location of the flange doublers.

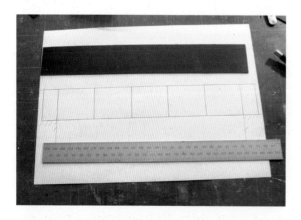

The basic web of the bridge is drawn to scale. The abutments are shown in the cross-hatched areas. The abutments are set at the carriage width. The bridge's span is increased by the amount bearing on the abutments. The web is then divided into panels.

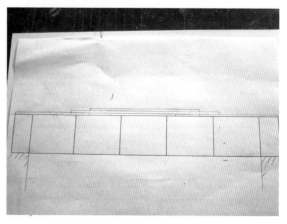

The doubling flanges have been drawn on to the top flange. They have been drawn considerably thicker than scale simply to make them show clearly on the drawing.

CONSTRUCTION

CONSTRUCTING THE GIRDER

Once the leading dimensions have been determined, the webs were cut from 0.040in plasticard. I have used black plasticard in this structure simply to make subsequent additional parts show clearly in contrast when illustrating the construction; there is no particular need to use it. One drawback is that locations cannot be drawn on in pencil – they have to be lightly scribed on to the surface.

The positions for the web spacers scribed into the surface. When scribing, greater care has to be exercised, a line in the wrong place may show up. Unlike a pencil line, scribed lines cannot be rubbed out. The opposite side also has had lines scribed for other details to be added.

The edge flanges were then prepared and were also cut from 0.040in plasticard. They have to be stuck to the web equally each side. The easiest way is to scribe two guide lines not quite to the centre of the strip leaving the web thickness between the lines. This serves to make a clear alignment for the web. The flange is then joined to the web using the lines to guide the position.

To ensure the flanges dried square to the web, both girders were placed side by side. Steel rules were placed along the outer flanges of the pair supports square to the surface the girders were on.

Weights were pushed against them after an initial squeeze to push the flanges upright. The whole was then left for the adhesive to fully dry.

Once the end flanges have been attached, the doubling flanges can be added to the top and bottom flanges. The edges of the flanges do not have to be blended and hidden as they are quite apparent on the prototype.

The flange strip cut out and the web position marked. The lines were scribed by setting the dividers to the appropriate dimension to leave the gap in the middle. One leg was run down the edge, whilst the other scribed the line. This is easier than trying to mark the position at each end and aligning a straight edge on a narrow strip of material.

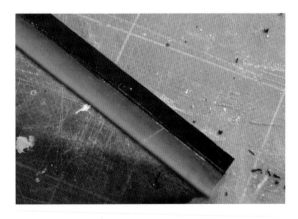

The first flange added. The scribed line is just visible at the joint. The other edges have their flanges added in a similar way. This can be done by eye, but a final straightening of the web along the flange may be necessary. Fitting a straight edge into the corner and pushing the web to it will do the job.

The girder assemblies set up whilst the glue dried. The two blocks have been cut and sanded from hardwood with all the sides nominally square. They are part of my tool kit. Items like this are useful tools in many applications. The weights come from old kitchen scales, spare ones in my case, but could be 'borrowed' from the kitchen under other circumstances.

The first top doubler has been added, the second one waits fixing. The sketch shows the arrangement.

DETAILING THE BASIC GIRDER

All the flanges now need their rivet detail added. For the size of the flanges there need to be four rows of rivets along the riveted strips. Prototypically all the rivets in the rows are side by side. My riveting tool can produce long runs of equally spaced rivets, but placing a second row with side-by-side rivets is impossible because of its indexing arrangement. Other tools have more accurate indexing that should allow this; however, I do not think this essential as the overall effect of having the rivets is convincing enough.

The rivets have been embossed into 0.030in plasticard. I have found that thicker plasticard distorts dramatically when embossed due to the amount of material displaced in the process. The model illustrated is to 7mm:1ft scale; for smaller scales the thickness should be reduced.

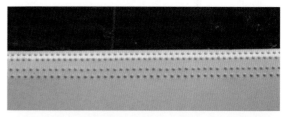

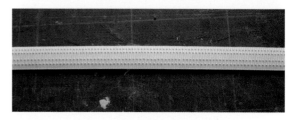

Rivets are embossed along the edge of a sheet of 0.030in plasticard. The embossing process has stretched the material and caused the curve across the lines. The strip is then cut from the sheet. The curve can be mostly removed by gently pulling the strip through the fingers, flattening it. Any residual curve will be lost when it is stuck down.

A riveted strip being offered up before fixing. The process is repeated on all the flanges. The strip is cut half-way between the rivets. Chopping with the scalpel is easier than trying to draw the blade across the strip in this instance.

The girders with rivet detail added to the flanges. Although the rivets are not side by side as they should be, the long lines of rivets take the eye away from this detail.

The strip is cut to length, flattened and then attached on top of the web flanges. The strip needs to be cut carefully between the rivets.

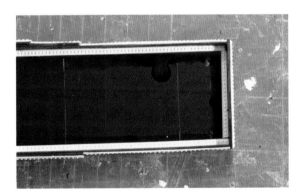

The single row strips added to the web inside the girder. These have to go on before other details on the web are added.

The next step is to fit single-row strips of rivets around the inside on the web faces. I fitted these to the outside only because I felt that adding strips to the inner faces was not worthwhile as they cannot be easily seen. Similarly, I have not added a riveted finish to the inside of the flanges as I felt it would look too cluttered.

The web supports are fitted next. The ones at the ends are a different form from the ones in the middle – they have a full-depth web rather than a reduced one. This is cut as a strip and then the inside

corners trimmed at 45 degrees to clear the rivet strip. On the prototypes this would be bent from a single piece of material forming the attachment to the web and the flanges. On the model it is easier to make from individual pieces suggesting it is one component.

The end web support fitted. The clearance angles can be seen beside the rivet strip. A scrap of riveted strip has been used to cut out a single rivet on a square base to fix to the flange at the end of the support. A single row strip completes the item.

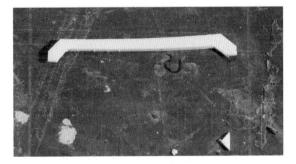

One of eight web supports cut out in the manner described, a series of cuts. When making parts like this it is not unusual to have failures, so be prepared to make more. The slightly ragged edge is cleaned up by scraping with the scalpel blade. Note the small triangle, a trimmed outside corner. The background is not my best cutting mat!

The first reduced profile support fitted. It awaits the rivet strip and flange fittings.

The riveted strip and end fittings added. The strip could have been better butted to the support. It is supposed to represent a single right-angled section.

The other web supports have a reduced profile. On the prototype they are formed from angle sections, sometimes with the web forged to clear the riveted strip, others are cut away as the end support. The smaller supports were cut from 0.030in plasticard as this is easier to work than thicker material. Sections were cut the depth of the web and the width of the flange. The shape was cut out using a scalpel to first chop off the corners, then parallel cuts were made into the edge above the ends. These cuts were then joined within the strip. The resulting shape can be seen in the illustration.

Each of the supports is fixed alongside the earlier scribed lines. A single riveted strip is stuck alongside. To the left of the girder the strips are stuck on the right-hand side of the support and on the other half to the left. Though there is no fixed rule as to which side they fit as long as one half mirrors the other.

The girder is completed by adding riveted strips on the inside face, which represent doublers to the support fixing rivets. There could be further web gussets if it were a higher loaded bridge.

THE BRIDGE DECK

A simple deck has been modelled for this bridge, which consists of a track support plate and cross-girders with brick jack arches between. An alternative could have been cross-girders with longitudinal girders supporting longitudinal timber baulks with the track in bridge chairs. This is like the earlier illustrated truss-girder bridge.

The width of the deck is for a single track. The length is a little more than the length of the girders to allow for matching into the trackbed either side of the abutments. This has been cut from 0.080in plasticard. It needs to be stiff to prevent it distorting when the girders and jack arches are added.

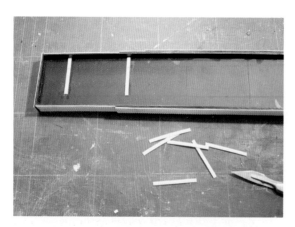

The doubling strips added on the inside. Note they stop short of the bottom of the girder on the horizontal scribed line. This line is the top of the bridge deck. The distance above the bottom flange is determined by adding up the depth of the cross-girder plus the thickness of the deck.

The deck marked out for the cross-girders. There are three lines at each girder position. The middle one is the centreline of each girder. As this will be hidden when positioning the girder, a line each side of it has been marked showing the edges of the girder flanges.

Rolling the brick around a tube. Note the tube is a lot smaller than the final radius. Making it tighter allows for the material to spring back to a radius closer to the final one. Heating with a hair drier softens the plastic, encouraging it to curve. The horizontal mortar courses help too.

The spacing of the cross-girders was determined by trial and error. A strip of the embossed brick plasticard was formed to make a small arch that fitted between the bottom edges of the cross-girder and no higher than the girder – this determined the width of the brick strip.

The girders, from Plastruct section, are stuck down on the marked positions, which have to be

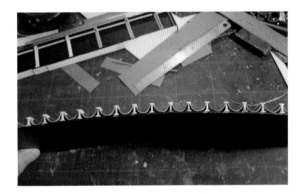

Here all the arches are in place. Note that the deck has taken on a curve. This was remedied by flattening – quite simply a rule across the top with a weight on it pressing the deck flat.

The brick being inserted between the girders. Note the alignment of the bricks. The brick has to be shaped to make it easier to fit, otherwise it will tend to jam. The slight curve in the illustrated part is insufficient to make it fit.

accurately cut to length and care taken to ensure that the ends of the girders are flush with the edges of the deck. If there is an overlap then the girders cannot be securely attached.

Once secure the brick sections can be added between the girders. The brickwork in the arches is in stretcher bond with the length of the bricks across the width of the deck. A degree of forming is required to make the brick fit between the girders. Rolling it around a brass tube with simple force from fingers can be sufficient, but warming with a hair drier can help.

Under the press. A rule and a kitchen weight serves to flatten the assembly. After about twenty-four hours the bend was negligible. Note that the two end spaces do not have arches fitted. These are on top of the abutments and so out of sight.

The brick arches can be fitted quite quickly. This results in bending of the deck, which can be removed by pressing the deck flat for a period of time.

Once the deck is flat it needs two curbs fitted on the upper surface to stop the ballast sitting against the girder webs. This prevents corrosion on the girder from the water that is held in the ballast. The curbs were made from a laminate of two pieces of 0.030in plasticard, one of which has a line of rivets along one edge to suggest the construction of the curb once the majority of it is hidden by ballast. The height of the curb should be similar to the thickness of the sleepers of your trackwork.

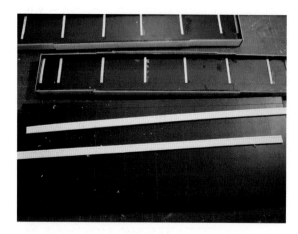

The two curbs ready to be fixed to the deck. A scribed line marks the position along the edge of the deck. This is set in from the edge around a scale 12–18in (30–45cm).

JOINING THE DECK AND GIRDERS

With both curbs fitted the deck can be fixed to the girders. The cross-girders sit on the flange of the main plate girder with jack arches butted to the web of the girder. The girder needs to be supported upright whilst fixing.

Initially adhesive is run along the top of the deck edge against the girder. This is most accessible as

The curbs are in position. The deck is now ready to be fixed to the girders. The scribed lines visible are an earlier error when marking out for the jack arches.

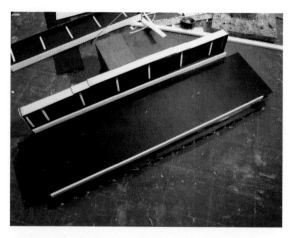

The first girder being fitted to the deck. Note the block behind the girder supporting it while the adhesive cures. At this stage it is easiest to apply the adhesive from the top only. Trying to turn it upside down before the joint has cured is likely to displace the parts.

The second girder added. The girders and jack arches can be seen inside the bottom edge of the first girder. At this stage the whole assembly can be turned upside down and further adhesive added along all the jack arches and cross-girders, enough to make a thorough bond between the deck and girders.

the deck is resting on the girder flange. Once the first girder is secure, the second can be fixed. Again adhesive is applied from the top. When cured, the whole assembly can be inverted and adhesive applied around the jack arches and cross-girders against the main girder web to ensure a thorough joint.

THE ABUTMENTS AND WING WALLS

The basic construction of the abutments and wing walls has been made in the same manner as those shown in the chapter on the masonry arch bridge. I do not propose to repeat the description. The parts are made up as hollow sections.

The difference in construction between the wing walls and abutments for this bridge and the earlier one is that they are finished with embossed stonework. Like the brickwork this is a Slater's product. The stone sheets come with an uneven edge that prevents easy edge-to-edge matching and so it has to be trimmed. Similarly, when using the sheets they need to be oriented so they are the same way up.

A set of abutments and wing walls. These have been made in 0.040in plasticard with spacers between.

Two sheets of embossed stonework nominally aligned. The large blocks two rows high can be seen at the top and lower half of each sheet. These make quick reference points. The left-hand sheet shows the need for the bottom edge to be trimmed; both show the need for trimming to match on the vertical join.

Putting the sheets side by side enables the courses to be aligned. The large, double-course stones help as reference points on this particular sheet.

ADDING THE STONEWORK

The abutment was the first item to receive its stonework. The main wall was flooded with adhesive, softening the surface and making it sticky. The stonework was treated in the same way but a little more cautiously. The hollows should not be allowed to collect the adhesive in puddles because this will make them extremely soft and any pressure will collapse them. When both surfaces are judged to be sufficiently sticky, bring them together with enough overlap either side to fold the stonework on to the sides of the abutment.

Once located and the adhesive dry the sides can be folded around the corners. Unlike the brickwork, the heavy embossing does not respond to simple scoring but requires the stones to be cut and the horizontal mortar courses to be cut. This is not easy and it is quite likely that the sheet will be cut through in its entirety. Do not worry; just remember the courses need to be aligned when sticking it in place. If you are successful and the sheet remains nominally in one piece, then fold it around the corner. The initial cutting and scoring may not be enough, so repeat until the stonework folds easily. Treat the surfaces with adhesive as before to make them sticky. Note that the stonework needs to be trimmed later to fix the wing walls, so do not go too far down the side of the abutment with the adhesive.

ABOVE: *The stonework has been folded around the corner and the voids of the opened-up stones can be clearly seen. For the time being these are left open.*

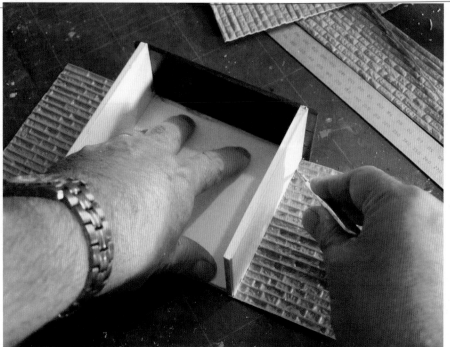

LEFT: *The stones have been stuck to the front of the abutment and the scoring and cutting is being made along the corner to enable the stonework to be folded around.*

When making the fold you will notice that the stones bulge, showing a void; this can be filled later, when the wing walls have been assembled to the abutment, and it becomes invisible.

The wing walls are covered with the stonework in the same manner using a covering of adhesive to make the surfaces sticky. The size of these wing walls mean that a pair could be nested on to one sheet making more economical use of a sheet. The bottom edge of the wall carcass was aligned with a horizontal mortar course. The continuity of the course one side to the other is not important. When fitted to the abutment, the courses will not match due to the batter of the wall. The discrepancy between one side and the other should not be noticed as it is very difficult to follow the course through due to the bridge obscuring the view.

Cutting the walls free. Note that the scalpel has run awry, fortunately in this case not into the stonework of the wall. On heavily embossed material like this it is more difficult to keep a blade under control due the deep relief.

Two wing walls and one sheet of stone. The bottom edge is aligned with a horizontal mortar course. The displacement of one wall to the other shows why the courses will not match across the bridge.

Once the stone is bonded to the carcasses, it is a simple matter to cut around the profile to release them.

The wing walls are now offered up to the abutment to determine what stonework has to be trimmed from the sides of the abutment. The slope of the wall is generally around 1 in 8, so that is the angle to aim for, if freelancing a bridge like this. For a prototype, then the true batter can be followed.

Only one wall has to be offered up and its slope marked. This can then be measured and repeated for the other positions.

A cut is made down each line and the stonework behind the line is removed. If minimal adhesive has been used, as described earlier, then the excess material can be easily stripped. There may be a bond in places but this will be on the mortar course lines and a blade can be inserted to cut the stonework free.

A wing wall positioned and a line drawn on the abutment. The stonework behind the wall on this line has to be removed from the abutment.

The top and bottom positions of the line are measured in order to be repeated on to the other sides of the abutment.

A cut has been made along the marked line and the stonework stripped away. The reason for not being too generous with adhesive can now be seen: most has come away cleanly but apparent are two patches that are more firmly secured. Residual bond can be seen below the upper patch. Fortunately the bond is only along the mortar courses, so a blade can be inserted to cut the remains free.

The wing walls can now be joined to the abutments. In this situation they have been fitted square to the abutment, in other words parallel to the carriageway; this is common in the urban situation. If the joint needs to be reinforced, then scrap strips can be bonded to the inside corner. If there is gap between the stones on the wall and the abutment do not worry as this can be dealt with at the same time as the gaps on the corners.

Pilasters and coping stones complete the abutments. The pilasters were made as described earlier, in this case a box of 0.080in plasticard to the required size, which were covered in the embossed stone. Their caps were made from three thicknesses of the

One wing wall bonded to the abutment. The stone courses in this joint nominally line up, but not always. Note the gap at the joint; this can be filled later.

A completed abutment with pilasters and coping stones. The coping stones have been similarly treated to the capping stones to roughen their surfaces.

0.80in plasticard. Once the adhesive had cured, they were squared up and chamfer cut along the edges. The finished cap was then attached to the body of the pilaster and the pilasters were then attached to the abutments. Some trimming of the abutment top was needed to achieve this – a lack of forward planning here.

The final task is to fill the gaps and holes. For this I use DIY filler, often Polyfilla or other equivalent. It is mixed to the consistency of thick cream and applied with a brush to the whole surface. Use the brush to force the filler into the holes and gaps, and spread the filler across all the stonework in a thin layer. This adds further texture to and removes the shiny finish to the plasticard. When the filler is dry the surface is sealed with matt emulsion. For colour I prefer magnolia rather than white as this can be too stark.

A pilaster in position with its capping stone. Again there are holes at the corners. The surface of the capping stone has been roughened by the application of a ball-ended cutter in the modelling drill. This is lightly scribbled across the surface.

ABOVE: **The filler and a mixed batch of filler in the mug. If you use a mug or similar household container remember to clean it thoroughly to remain popular in the household.**

LEFT: **The filler being brushed on. Use a bristle brush to spread the filler, the stiffness of the bristles is an advantage. Work the filler into the holes and gaps, then paint it over the surface.**

This completes the construction of the bridge. Painting the girders and stonework is all that remains. This is covered in Chapter 11.

ABOVE: **On the coping and cap stones, stipple the surface filler with the brush to keep the rough texture.**

LEFT: **The whole surface has now been covered in filler and awaits its coat of emulsion paint.**

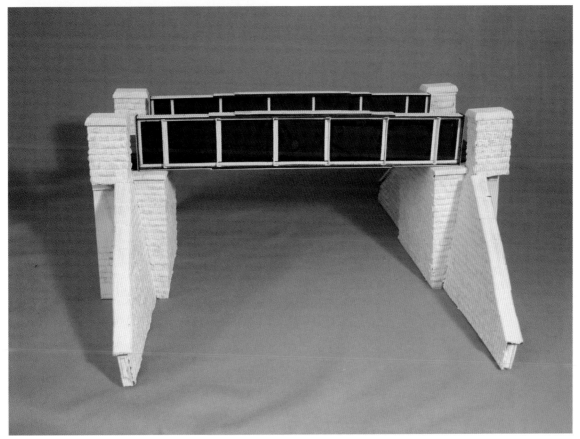

The completed bridge just awaiting painting.

CHAPTER TEN

A VIADUCT

THE PROTOTYPE

When I set out to make the model viaduct, the aim was to make something based on Midford Viaduct on the Somerset and Dorset line. I had been supplied with a curved board by a friend on which to build the model; it is intended for his railway. However, the best laid plans... Midford Viaduct consists of eight arches on a shallow curve. The board supplied has a radius of 8ft (2.4m) and there was only room for four arches. As a consequence the viaduct made is one that suits the situation.

Over the years I have previously made three other viaducts, this being the fourth. All have been built on a curve. I would suggest that this may be the most common form on a model railway, as there is often little room for a straight one. Besides which, making one on the straight is far more straightforward than a curved one.

Midford Viaduct set amongst trees. The trees made it very difficult to get a clear view of much of the structure to enable a photographic record of the structure to assist the build of the potential model. This is not an uncommon situation for older structures that are no longer in use.

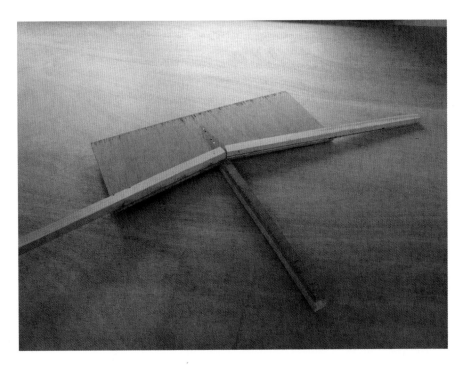

The centre finder tool. The angle between the two legs of the V is around 160 degrees, for a smaller radius it can be smaller. The dividing leg is set at half the angle. One edge is the line that makes half the angle. A piece of 6mm ply has been used to make the foundation of the tool and a further piece added to the dividing leg to make up the thickness of the foundation piece.

THE MODEL

Unlike the prototype, which is built from the piers up and then arches turned, I have found it easier to build a model from the top down. The trackbed makes a foundation for the rest of the structure to be built on. The model is built to a scale of 7mm:1ft and uses 12mm ply as the trackbed. I would suggest that even in the smaller scales this thickness of ply be used as it is thick enough to accept fixings into the edge without the worry of it splitting.

In this instance the trackbed was cut to match the curve of the board supplied. When the ply was cut it was marked out using a pencil attached to a batten at the required radius from a nail as the centre pivot. In this case the centre of the radius was not on the board it was cut from, so once the trackbed was marked out, the centre was lost.

To mark out the arches you need to know at least the radial direction of the centre from the curve. A simple tool was made to mark out the radial lines, consisting of two pieces of wood joined together to form a shallow 'v' and a third that divides the angle between them.

CONSTRUCTION

SETTING OUT

The trackbed was marked out with the centre finder. First, the ends of the viaduct were defined, a certain distance in from each end. The length around the

Using the measured mark, the centre finder is pressed against the edge and a line drawn across the trackbed to mark the centre of a pier. The tool has been moved aside to show the line clearly but the fit of the two arms to the edge can be seen.

outside edge of the trackbed was measured. A tape is ideal for this as it will flex around the curve. The measured length was then divided into four; these positions are the centrelines of each pier. Using the measured marks, the tool is then used to draw a radial line across the board.

An arch centreline marked with a dashed line.

Once the pier positions are marked, the centres of each arch have to be found. The distances between the centrelines is halved and marked. The tool is again used to draw a line across the trackbed – in this case a dashed line to differentiate it from the other lines.

With the basic dimension set out, the size of the piers can be determined. As this structure was not following the scale dimensions of any prototype, it was a matter of making the proportions correct.

An arch on a curved viaduct has parallel sides, it does not taper; the pier tapers across the trackbed like a wedge of cheese. The inner and narrowest end of the pier cannot be too narrow. Prototypically it can be no narrower than the thickness where two sets of arch rings meet on top of the pier. If there are only five rings of brick, this can be somewhat spindly. A width scaling of 6½ft (2m) looked good without the outer wider end looking too fat.

Using the arch centreline the position of the arch was marked out.

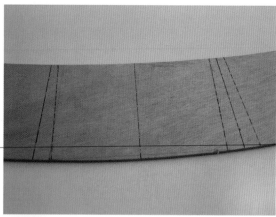

ABOVE: **The illustration shows one pier and the end of the arch highlighted in felt-tip pen over more accurate marking that can be just made out in the chord line on the outer edge. The chord line is drawn between the pier centrelines and is used to mark the sides of the arch.**

LEFT: **The trammels have been set to the width of the arch (they could be compasses or dividers for smaller dimensions) from the width at the narrow end of the pier, and using the intersection of the arch centreline and the chord line, the sides are marked at the wider end of the pier. The marks are joined up giving two parallel sides and a tapering pier.**

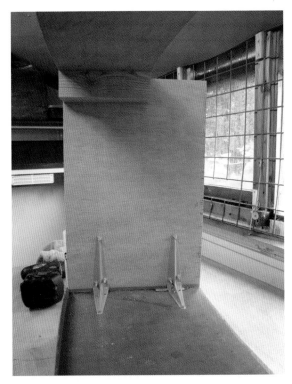

The original baseboard with the green original surface has been modified by the addition of end plates. The brackets supporting one of the end plates can be seen. Above is the new trackbed with blocks of wood to locate it. At this stage the blocks are only fitted to the trackbed. It will be joined to the end plate when the structure is completed.

SETTING UP THE TRACKBED

The original baseboard was modified by having its ends extended upwards and a ply plate was added at each end, supported by shelf brackets bolted on. Something similar could be done for a new construction as the board housing the viaduct will be deeper than the others. The new trackbed sits on these end plates and is located by a block of wood at each end. The blocks could not be added until after the trackbed had been marked out, as they would stop lying flat.

MARKING AND CUTTING OUT THE ARCHES

When all the arches and piers have been marked out, the positions along both the inner and outer edges of the trackbed are now known. These can be transferred on to the material that becomes the sides – I have used 0.080in plasticard for this. Unlike the construction of the earlier bridges, I have not made a cavity wall structure. In this thickness of material, in combination with the curvature, it will be stable. I have cut the sides from a single large sheet of plasticard (1350 × 660mm – nominally 4 × 2ft) to keep them as one piece. Slater's Plastikard Ltd was the supplier in this case.

With the basic dimensions derived, the plasticard can now be marked out. To avoid problems placing the point of the circular cutter on the very edge of the plasticard, a line 6mm from the edge was drawn. The centres of the arches were marked out and the curves drawn.

After the arches, the top edge of the parapet is marked and also the line of the top surface of the trackbed – this is important as it is the datum for

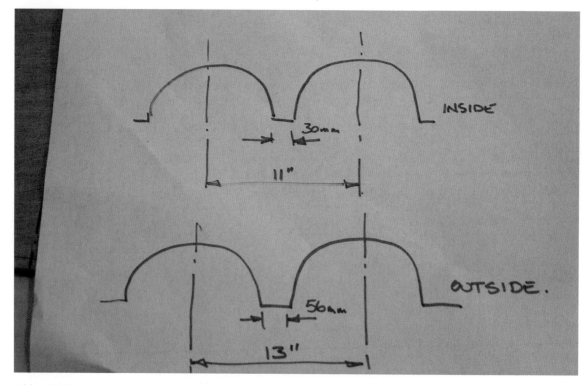

A sketch showing the basic dimensions of the arches. I offer no apologies for mixing the units; the longest ones were most conveniently expressed in inches and the smaller ones in millimetres. Sometimes it is easier to use them this way, as expressed inches the number is small, whereas in millimetres it is large and because of the smaller divisions greater chance of miscounting on the rule.

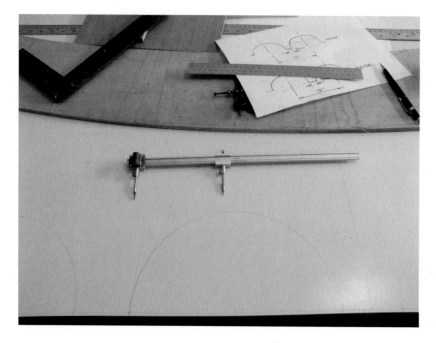

The arches are initially marked out in pencil. This is better than scribing as errors can easily be erased. Of course, the pencil lines do not lend themselves to showing clearly in a photograph.

All the essential marking done: arches, top of parapet, trackbed datum highlighted with the arrow and the lower line for the fixing holes.

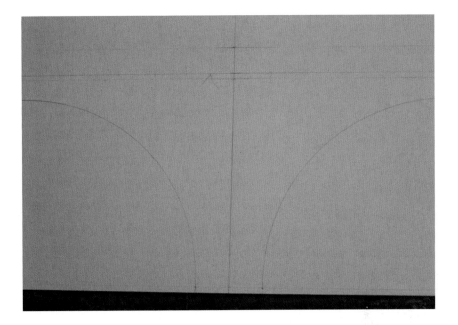

securing the side to the trackbed, and below that line, by half the thickness of the trackbed plywood, a line to mark the horizontal position of the holes for fixing the side to the ply.

Cutting the arc of the arch is done with the modified blade in the trammels. This scrapes a thin line of plastic away so, having thickness unlike a blade cut, it needs to be set inside the previously marked pencil line. Once there is a groove, then that can used to guide a scalpel around the curve. The unwanted material can be broken out by flexing the plasticard across the cut.

The inside of the arc will have a burr, which should be removed by running a scalpel blade around the edge. It will remove the burr in preference to cutting into the thickness of the plasticard.

Scoring around the arc. A series of cuts are needed on thicker plasticard. It is not necessary to cut all the way through. It is enough to create a groove half-way through the thickness and then finish the cut with a scalpel.

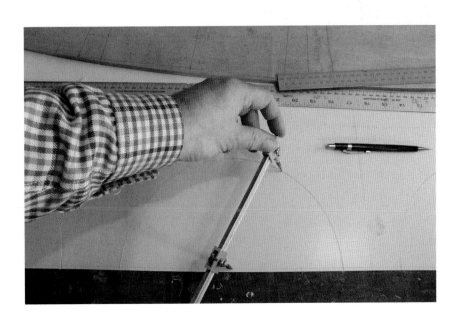

Once the cut has been made, then the unwanted plasticard can be broken out. Flexing the part backwards and forwards will advance the break.

The side is then cut from the main sheet. As this is a long cut it has to be done with care. A series of cuts is made along the line from one end to the other. These are deepened progressively until about half-way through. All the cuts are done using a straight edge but once the cut is established it will guide a blade, provided it is pulled in a straight line. There is a tendency when using a blade freehand that you can take it around a radius based on the length of your arm. Once partially cut through, the side can be broken away from the main sheet by flexing it over an edge, for example a table edge.

All the arches cut out and the straight cut about to be made.

FITTING THE SIDES

Once the side has been separated from the main sheet, then the holes that take screws to fix it to the trackbed can be drilled. They need to be relatively close together to ensure the side fits snugly to the trackbed. Drill and countersink them to match the screws.

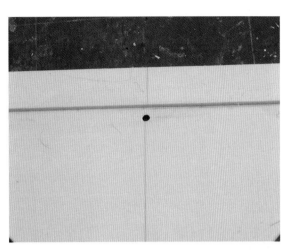

A detail of the strip fixed to the top of the side. This has been cut from the same thickness of plasticard as the side (0.080in) to double the thickness of the parapet and provided a locating edge to the trackbed.

The holes have been drilled about 3in (75mm) apart. Rather than a jobber's drill I have used a 'slocum' or lathe centre drill to make the holes. This starts with a small diameter and then progressively increases. It will cut without 'chatter' or having the flutes of the drill hang up in the hole and tearing the material. The holes are then countersunk for the screw head. Check each one to ensure the head sits below the surface. This is important to prevent them showing when the brick overlay is added.

Temporarily fit the inner side aligning the centres of the piers and with a radial line from the end of the outer to the inner mark the inner side where the line touches. Trim the end to this line.

Fit the inner side as before.

Once the holes have been drilled, a strip is cut to the width between the top of the side and the level of the trackbed. This is stuck in place. It serves not only to double the thickness of the parapet but also to locate the side on top of the trackbed.

Once the adhesive has dried then the side can be fitted to the trackbed. Start with the outside part as it is longer than the inner. Put the first screw in the middle and move towards the ends – this will prevent small buckles appearing. Pilot drill the trackbed for the screws so they can be tightened easily.

Having fitted one side, the second follows. It will be necessary to trim the ends to match the outside.

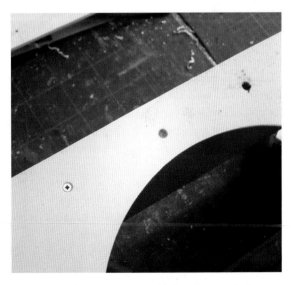

The first screw in place with its head sitting below the surface so it will not show under the succeeding brick overlay. The same holds for them all.

The two sides fitted to the trackbed making a flat 'H'-section girder. This has some structural stability even at this stage.

STIFFENING THE SIDES

Now, having a basic structure, it requires stiffening. To do this braces are fitted between the sides. These were strips about 20mm (¾in) wide cut from the semi-circular pieces that made the arches and to the width of the trackbed. They are bonded across the structure nominally placed as follows: one at the top of the arch, one at each 45-degree position on the arch and one each side at the bottom of the arch. Unless the strips are exactly tailored to the position, the curvature will give a small gap on part of one end. This can be overcome by adding a small piece of the strip to make a gusset. These will come from the trimmings removing the residual arcs from the ends of the strips.

The stiffening has been added around the arches. The strips at the bottom of the arches are vertical with only the bottom edges touching the edge of the arch. The small gussets at the ends of the strips can be seen. When the brickwork for the arch is glued in it will be attached around the arch and along the edge of the bottom stiffeners.

ADDING THE ARCHES AND ELECTRICS

When I first inserted the brick arch, it was a failure. I initially added a skin of 0.030in plasticard to form the arch and then added a second skin of the brick embossed plasticard. The bond between the two was very poor resulting in arches with a series of irregular flats – they were removed and scrapped. Sometimes you have to be ruthless. Removal was, by and large, easy as the bond around the arch was still soft, so running blade around the joint separated the parts. However, in some places the bond was better

and residual plastic had to be ground away with a sanding drum in the modelling drill.

It was at this point I realized that I had not made any provision for the power supply to the tracks. The length of the trackbed means that it will take more than one yard of track to complete the span. Rather than relying on fishplates at the joints, it is better to provide a positive feed to the rails from a separate supply.

The first version of the arch needed the sheets to be joined. In part the in situ joining led to the problems.

Two wires were laid from one end to the other. They terminate in a small choc block connector at each end. At each arch position, two holes were drilled through the trackbed and wires passed through and joined into the main feed. A generous length was left on the top to connect to the, as yet unlaid, track. The stiffener at the top of the arch had to be cut to accommodate the wire. It has been fixed to the trackbed using a bead of glue from a hot glue gun. Once that had set, the gap was cut. The hot glue also secures the wires to the trackbed. Note the black plasticard strip around the arch. This has been placed to make good unevenness in the arch following removing residual plastic from the first arch.

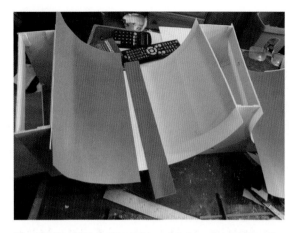

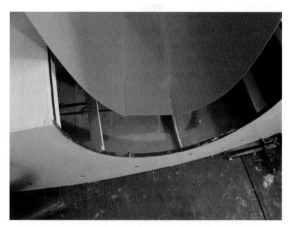

The original brick skin being added to the 0.030in liner. It can be seen that three pieces of plasticard are needed to fit the arch. Bonding, or failing to bond, the brick to liner caused the problems. A single skin of brick was the solution. This was again three pieces but they were joined with small lapping strips in 0.020in plasticard. These did not go the full width of the arch, stopping short of the sides. The narrower strip of brick was made wider than its earlier equivalent, which enables it to bend more freely. The whole piece was pushed into the archway and glued from middle to sides, pressing it in place as the bond became sticky.

When all the arches were in place and the glue set, they were trimmed to width. The point of a scalpel blade was run around the brick, guided by the side of the structure. This was done several times until light could be seen through the plasticard. The blade was then applied to the edge of the plasticard from inside the arch and pushed along the scored line, again guided by the side.

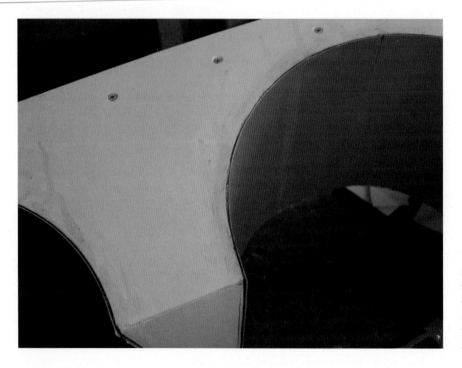

The brick skin trimmed back to the edge of the sides. The bottom edges have been cut in the same way as the ends, using the structure as a guide.

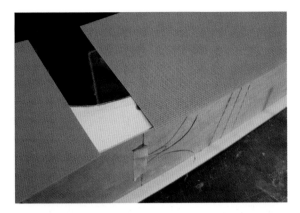

Planning the joint at the top of the arch. One of the pairs of wires to the track can be seen.

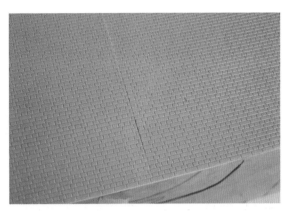

A joint between two sheets. The apparent gap can be reduced by the addition of a little more adhesive and the plasticard pressed down with a spatula. The handle of a scalpel does this well. A little plastic filler may help provided it is not used in such quantity as to blind the embossing.

ADDING THE BRICK TO THE SIDES

A number of sheets of embossed brick are needed to cover the sides and this means there will be joins. If the joins are arranged to occur near the top of the arch, then there will be fewer number of brick courses to align. The sheets need to be trimmed to a give an appropriate consistent course along the top and to match the sheets side by side. The cut edges will have a small burr, especially on the vertical joints: scrape the scalpel blade along and across the corner of the edge to remove this.

The brick is stuck to the side by first flooding adhesive over the side to create a soft surface; this is repeated on the brick and the two joined. The edge of the parapet was used as the datum for the top row of bricks. The surface was prepared for the next sheet and that added; this time the alignment with the top and the brick courses of the earlier sheet have to be made.

When all the sheets are stuck to the sides they have to be trimmed. Again a scalpel is run around the profile from the inside of the arch. It helps to have a small block of MDF or similar to press the blade into as the blade moves around otherwise the sheet may be lifted from the side. A block is safer than fingers. The incomplete cut can be seen running around to the top of the pier. Note the small amount of filler on the joint between the sheets at the top of the arch.

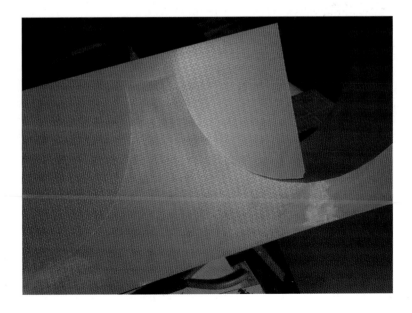

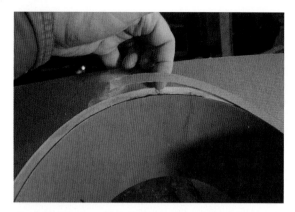

The sides have been cut through following the scoring. The ring is then lifted away, though a little help with a blade underneath may be needed. The edge of the arch may need a little trimming to ensure it is flush. The area just below the finger is a little proud.

The first ring in place. Inevitably there are joints in the strips, so when the second and subsequent strips are added, ensure they alternate from side to side. The final strip may be a tight fit but, using the handle of a scalpel, it can be pushed into place.

COMPLETING THE ARCH AND SIDES

The ends of each arch have to be completed with the brick rings that make the arch structure. For this arch there are five rings of brick: the brick on the side of the arch has to be removed to accept these rings. Using a pair of dividers, the points are set five courses apart. This can be picked off from the embossed sheet. The dividers are then run around the edge of the arch scoring a groove in the brick around the arch. The groove is then cut through and a ring of brick removed. The adhesion of the brick to

the side should not be sufficient to prevent the brick from being easily lifted away.

Having cut away the horizontal courses of brick around the arch, the ring courses need to be added. These are cut from the embossed sheet, taking the headers from between the stretchers of the English bond. With practice they can be cut out with a point of a scalpel blade run down the mortar course without the aid of a straight edge. The complementary stretcher courses have to be discarded.

The first ring is attached beside the arch using

The rings have been completed with some filler and the string course is being added. Note the carved edges to the stones and the small bevel at the ends.

the arch to guide the strip. A degree of pre-forming can be done by running the strip through the fingers 'persuading' it to bend. The subsequent rings follow guided by the first. A little plastic filler may be needed to 'improve' the fit.

Once the rings are done, the string course below the parapet is added. This usually coincides with the base of the ballast on the trackbed. Rather than brick I have added a stone string course. A strip of 0.080in plastic was cut three brick courses high and long enough to fit the span. To create a rough effect the corners were carved, random removal of material along the length and the surface scored with coarse

wet and dry emery paper. The strips were then subsequently cut to scale 4ft (1.2m) lengths and the end bevelled by filing across the corner, just a couple of strokes. The individual stones were then stuck to the sides.

THE PIERS

The height of these piers means it would be very unlikely they would be straight-sided – a tapering pier is most likely. A slope around 2 degrees looked right, nothing more than a judgement.

Only three piers have been made, the centre one and one each side. When fitting the deck to the

A set of pier parts: ends and sides. The relative size between ends and sides can be seen. The greater width of the side requires the stiffening pieces added to stop it bowing when the brick is laminated on to it. Also seen down the edges are strips: one the tapering edge cut from a side and the other cut from a wider strip. These increase the area at the edges to bond the sides to the end. Two sides and an end joined. It helps to draw an outline of the planform of the pier to help line up the parts.

baseboard it became clear that the sides of the valley the viaduct spans would put the ends of the outer arches in the ground.

The ends of the piers were cut out using dimensions from the height of the viaduct and the width of the bases between the arches. The sides were cut out to fit between the ends and as long as the sloping side. Although these parts are assembled as a box, the sides are too flexible to be without some internal stiffening. This was made up with strips of plasticard 0.080in by 10mm wide cut from various off cuts. The edges have been doubled with strips to increase the area of attachment too.

The parts are joined together. As there are no right angles it is not possible to use a square to check the corners. Instead draw a plan of the foot of the pier and use that to guide the alignment of the parts. Once joined and the joints are set, it may be necessary to do a little touching up to the corners to get the parts in line. Using the side or end as a datum, surface file across the corner to remove any burrs or unevenness.

The brick was added to the piers next. Whole sheets were insufficient to cover in one go, so top and bottom edges had to be prepared to make the

joints. The sides were covered first. The surfaces of side and brick were prepared as before with the adhesive. Start at the top and add the second sheet below that, matching the brick courses.

Add the ends after the sides. Because of the taper in the pier, the trick of scoring and folding the brick

The brick has been stuck in place. The top edge is matched to the top edge of the side. The side is then cut to match the profile. The point of a scalpel is run down the edge to score it before cutting. Press the pier on to a surface whilst cutting. The resulting scores can be seen appearing on the outside surface. The excess material can be broken away or completely cut through.

The file is resting on the side, using that as a reference whilst it is cutting, to clean up burrs or any protruding edge. If it scores the surface, that does not matter as they will be hidden by the brick plasticard. Use the file to cut towards the body of the part, if cutting away there is a possibility of undoing the joint.

The corner after cutting. The alignment of the courses here is not perfect but not significantly so; once painted it will largely disappear against the size of the whole structure.

around the corner cannot be used, as the courses will not be horizontal across the end. The end has to be added after the side so that when it is trimmed it overlaps the side brick plasticard. The join will then be less apparent on the corner. The viaduct will be mostly seen from the side, presenting the ends of the piers to view.

JOINING THE PIER TO THE DECK

Once completed, the piers have to be secured to their positions under the deck – offer them up to see how they look. I have elected to use corbels to join the piers to the deck. Corbels are thicker sections of brickwork at the top of the pier stepping out from the base brickwork. A feature like this will be used in the construction of the arches to provide a location for the timbering the arch is built on.

The corbels are made from strips of 0.080 plasticard, six bricks wide, giving an overlap of three bricks on the deck and three bricks on the pier. The sides to the arch pieces have to be added first because of the taper in the pier. Once they are secured, then the ends can be added. Make them oversize, overlapping the side pieces. Once secure, trim to length then, following the side pieces, file the profile into the ends.

Add strips of brick plasticard over the sides overlapping the ends and trim to the outside of the ends.

Checking the piers under the deck. Already it has a presence.

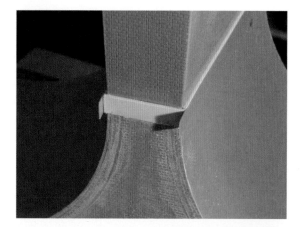

This hides the joint at the corners between the side and end pieces. Trim and complete with brick over the ends, trimming to match the side pieces.

To complete the viaduct, the capping stones and the interior walls of the parapet need to be added. Strips of 0.080in plasticard were cut to the length of each wall. A long strip will not curve to the top of the parapet, so needs to be cut to make it fit. The strip was cut into sections of scale 6ft (1.8m) long and each section cut and stuck to the top of the wall with equal overhangs. Start from each end to notionally meet in the middle and trim the final one to fit the remaining gap.

TOP: *The corbel being assembled. The two side strips are in place and the brick covering added. The small angle matching the taper of the pier can be made out to the left-hand side. The completing brickwork is to be added to the end. A further two brick strips are added to the top of the corbel.*

MIDDLE: *The corbel is completed with the second layer of two bricks added to the top. The pier is now well secured to the deck. The discoloration inside the arch is down to the adhesive.*

The capping strip added along the top of the parapet. The final rub down with coarse wet and dry has yet to be done. Note the final covering of brick has not yet been added to the end of the parapet.

When all the capping pieces are in place and secure, roughen them with coarse wet and dry to add some texture.

This completes the basic structure of the viaduct. All that remains is to set it in its valley. The structure has been primed with automotive acrylic primer as a base for subsequent finishing. The baseboard has had the sides of the valley added in hardboard. This is probably the best use for this material as it flexes readily to the curves of the baseboard and viaduct.

Two profiles in hardboard fixed at one end. The slope is quite steep, making a narrow valley. The profiles cut across the base at the end arches an be seen and shows why piers at the ends are not needed. From this the ground will be added.

CHAPTER ELEVEN

FINISHING

PAINT, BRUSHES AND FINGERS

PAINTS

I mostly use acrylic paints for my scenic and structural models, though the odd enamel paint does get used. The advantages of acrylic over enamel is the speed of drying; it very much faster and is virtually odour-free. The latter is something to consider when working in the household.

As base coat on plastic I use Halford's grey acrylic primer, which comes in an aerosol and can be sprayed on to give an even coat. The grey background makes unpainted areas obvious. If colouring brick on to brick-coloured plasticard, then patches can be missed. I have also found that it seems to protect the plastic from ageing. Some structures made a long time ago eventually crumbled; the plastic had deteriorated over time. I do not know why. Another building made round the same time and painted with the primer survives.

My favourite colour paints are from the Games Workshop Citadel range. Apart from black and white they come with some very strange-sounding names that, at best, only loosely describe the colour. Notwithstanding, there are several good earth colours. I usually choose by what appears in the transparent pot. To be sure I will often check the colour in daylight rather than under the shop lights. The store I buy from understands about this and I'm not accompanied to the door with a minder. Other shops may be different. The colours come in at least two types: there are the opaque 'base' colours and translucent ones that can be over painted on to the base colour; I stick with the base ones. They happily intermix.

An alternative is artist's acrylics. There is a huge range of these, nearly all going by recognized colour names, for example 'terracotta'. These can be a little harder to use because of their properties. Used direct from the tube they can go on thickly. This is a property that can be useful, but often I put the paint on a palette and use it from there with a little water in the brush or applied to a wetted surface. They dilute well and can be used as translucent

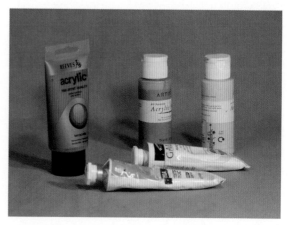

Pots of Citadel acrylic in various earth shades and red, yellow, black and blue. The blue is obviously used for blue brick but the other colours are also present in red brick walls. The artist's acrylic generally comes in tubes, but pots are equally useful and cheap.

A selection of brushes. The flat ones are good for brushing across flat surfaces as, if there is relief like mortar courses, they do not penetrate the crevices. All the ones illustrated have synthetic bristles. The orange coloured ones were from a high street shop selling discounted books and were very cheap. The quality is more than good enough for scenic painting.

washes over earlier colours, for example adding some green staining.

Enamel paints from Humbrol and Revel can be happily used instead of, and with, acrylics. They do not intermix but either can be painted on top of the other.

All the paints in pots need to be stirred or shaken to properly mix their contents. The acrylics respond to a good shaking and the enamels to a thorough stir. I have noticed on many models where enamel mixing has either not been done or done poorly, the paint does not cover and tends to dry glossy even when supposed to be matt.

BRUSHES

Always use the best brushes you can afford, though best sable hair is not necessary. In fact modern synthetic hair is, to me, better. The surfaces we work on can be quite abrasive so there is more wear on the brush.

The shape of the brush is important – a flat brush works better across a flat face than a round one. A flat brush held at a shallow angle on brickwork will leave paint without filling the mortar courses. Similarly, on a heavily textured stone surface it can be used to add paint on just the high spots. However, a small round brush can be used to pick out indi-

vidual bricks in different colours to add colour relief, deeper reds or browns and the odd black one.

FINGERS

Fingers can substitute for brushes; a patch of paint can be pressed into mortar courses to emphasize them. Alternatively, a damp finger can be used to wipe a surface to remove paint. To a degree, a fine-celled sponge, a synthetic one, can also do the same job.

PAINTING BRICKWORK

It pays to have a closer look at brickwork. The colour only looks uniform from a distance. Look back at some of the previous illustrations – the colours of individual bricks are all very different, even though they are generally described as red or blue. Red bricks can vary through orange to a deep red/brown, while blue bricks can vary from blue/grey to purple and black.

RED BRICK

I have chosen the masonry arch bridge made earlier to finish in red brick. This in spite of the fact that the prototype used was in blue brick! The nominally red brick plasticard has been sprayed with

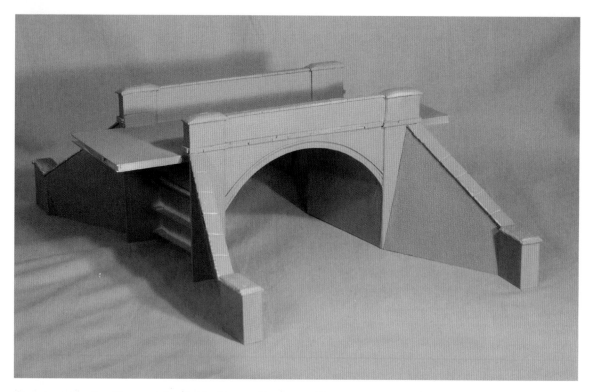

The starting point. The structure finished in acrylic primer. The coverage is not complete, the red plasticard is showing through in some places and some corners in plain have been missed, as access with an aerosol is not so easy without spraying far too much paint. This is not an issue.

acrylic primer, as have the stonework capping parts of the structure. The white plain plasticard has also received a coat too.

The base colours for the red brick are selected: there are several browns, an orange and red. All these are 'earth' colours. They are placed on to a palette to use – I have used a scrap of white card. Always use white as a base to mix on as any colour in the card can mislead the eye. A couple of brush-fuls of each colour are added to the palette in close proximity to each other. The colours will be mixed together but not evenly. Indeed not mixed together well at times. This can leave two colours on the brush to be applied to the model simultaneously.

Painting the Arch Bridge

With the selected colour on the brush, it is applied to the brickwork. The brush is held at a shallow angle

The palette: red, orange and brown in patches. A card palette like this enables you to unload the brush of excess paint before applying it to the model. The paint is mixed between the selected colours by pulling them into the middle to create the desired shade.

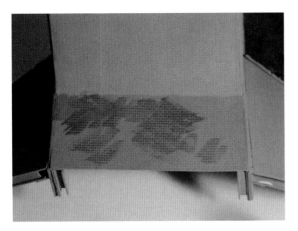

The colours being applied across the abutment and wing wall in cross shapes. The coverage is built up to complete the wall. The second picture shows the abutment nominally covered: the patches have run together and the start of the wing wall where thus far only a single direction has been done.

to the surface and stroked diagonally across the surface. The diagonal direction reduces the possibilities of filling the mortar crevices, as the brush does not align with the vertical and horizontals. Build up a series of Xs, changing the colour mix slightly each time across the face being painted. As the colour builds across the surface, small areas may not be covered, so search them out and cover them.

Once the colour has been built up across the surface, then individual bricks or small patterns of bricks can be picked out creating a patchwork of different colour. Contrasting colours are used to highlight the bricks, brighter orange, dark grey or black. A small, flat brush can be used if the end is close to brick sized or for smaller features, a small, round brush. A steady hand is needed.

Finishing the basic colour by pulling the brush across parts of the surface where bricks have been missed. Note the shallow angle of the brush.

TOP: *Individual and patterns of bricks are being picked out. In one area they are in orange and another in black. Some are grey. The overall brick colour has begun to be broken up.*

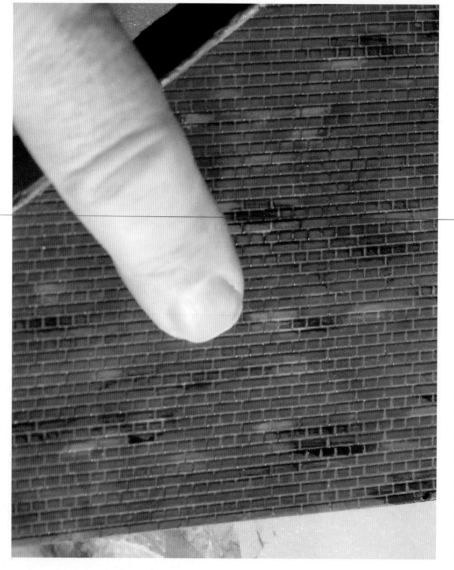

The black paint applied in the preceding picture is being pushed into a local area of mortar courses with the finger. The other bricks across the face have been re-coloured in places. Note that the colour across some bricks is incomplete, helping the patchwork effect.

Once the brickwork is complete, the stonework can be painted. This has been done in a grey that is close to the prototype bridge. As a bare colour this is too bland so it needs relieving by a wash of an alternate colour. For this I have used a brown. The edges of the individual stones have been picked out and then a further dilution has been washed across the surface. The wash will settle in the crevices created to roughen to surface and de-emphasize them.

The completed bridge is illustrated – all that remains is for it to be set in a scene.

ABOVE, ABOVE RIGHT AND RIGHT: **The stonework has been painted grey and then received a wash of brown on top. The enlarged detail shows how the wash stains the surface and fills the crevices.**

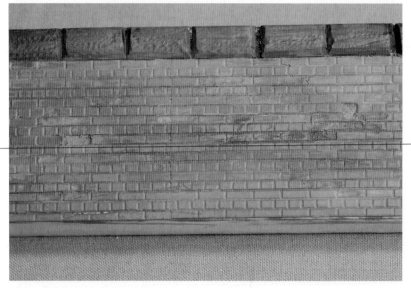

The abutments and central pier of the truss-girder bridge. The green wash shows around the bases. The enlargement of the pier shows the distressed bricks. These have a deeper orange colour than the others. Near the centre of the picture the join between two pieces of brick plasticard can just be made out.

Beside this bridge, brick abutments were made for the truss-girder bridge. These were heavily distressed as they were supposed to be made from a softer brick. Such softer bricks often have more orange hue than harder ones, a feature of the firing and clay used. These have been painted to represent this. In addition, as they will eventually end up in a river, so there is considerable green staining on the lower parts from the algae that grows in the damp conditions.

BLUE BRICK

Blue brick is perhaps more difficult to reproduce than red as it is not entirely blue. Though made from the same clay, the firing produces a range of colours that is more diverse in blue than red brick. These colours vary around a single brick too: there are deep reds, purples and a blackish blue. The way in which the brick is laid can emphasize the differences in colour.

A section of a blue brick wing wall showing the diversity of colours. All the headers have an even blue end; the stretchers vary between wholly deep red to partially red and blue.

If it were a small wall I would mix my palette using these colours. It helps to have a background to work on that is not the grey primer. The detail picture shows a test-piece to work out the method. The brickwork has been misted with black and blue from Citadel aerosol paints. The spray is directed at a very oblique angle to avoid filling the mortar courses; the same way as using the paint brush. You will note the

The three basic colours for blue brick, blue, red and black. Proportionally there is more blue and black than red. The second picture shows then being mixed together. The red has been used up to make a deep purple and then black is added.

The detail colours have been touched in on the misted surface, a little too much red in one spot, but the general effect can be seen.

The spandrel with its initial coat of black showing the uneven cover. Following this the blue has been added with the same effect.

mottled effect around the part that has not been treated in detail. The spray can was held at some distance from the brick to ensure incomplete coverage – the opposite to the usual objective of achieving complete cover.

Finishing the Viaduct

As can be seen in the illustrations, the viaduct has been primed. Following this I sprayed it as described above, alternating between the blue and the black mottling the surface.

ABOVE: **This shows the distance and angle a spray can is held to get the effect. The spray is being aimed at the left-hand arch in the picture; the distance of the can from the model is around 300–400mm (12–15in).**

RIGHT: **The wetted surface and paint filling the mortar courses. The paint is also in the film of water on top of the bricks, which as it dries, tones down the colour, lightening it.**

Different shades have been drawn across the brickwork to create a less uniform finish. A broad, flat brush has been used and drawn across the surface, transferring the paint to the surfaces of the bricks. Note the safety rails have been added.

Once the paint is dry you can go to work enhancing the effect. I added a light grey to fill the mortar courses. The surface was wetted and then a brush loaded with paint and drawn over the surface. The surface effect of the wetting draws the colour into the crevices.

The whole viaduct is reworked in this way and then further local colour changes have been added to reduce the uniformity of the brickwork. I have not done the detailed brick painting illustrated earlier – the structure is too large for this. It will be looked at from a distance so the refined approach can be modified to a more general effect.

THE SAFETY RAILS

The stanchions for the rails have been cut from 4mm bullhead rail. Lightweight rail is used prototypically on some bridges. The holes for the rail were

The stanchions fitted and a joint in the rail. The plastic filler has spread beyond the holes and needed cleaning off and subsequently the parapet had to be repainted.

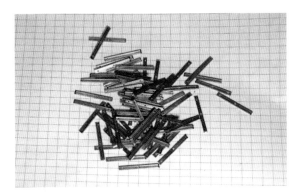

The rail has been cut into lengths: one end has been filed square and the other left sharp as the cutters left them. The rail has been drilled to accept the rail. To help with subsequent painting they have been chemically blackened.

drilled for the rail and then the stanchions chemically blackened with Birchwood Casey gun blue. I put the stanchions in a 35mm film cassette and poured the gun blue over them – the blackening takes less than a minute. The fluid is returned to its container and the parts spread out on a paper towel to dry them.

These have been spaced at a nominal scale 6ft (1.8m) apart. The positions were walked off from each end with a pair of dividers. Inevitably, somewhere near the middle the spacing goes awry. The spacing has been 'adjusted' by eye near the middle, slightly wider apart rather than closer together.

The diameter of the drill is chosen to match the height of the rail. The rail should be a tight-ish press-fit in the hole. The hole should be a little deeper than needed to allow some adjustment to the finished height of the stanchion. The first three stanchions were fitted into the holes with some plastic filler. The cut end that was left on the rail goes into the hole. It is sharp and slightly wider than the hole so cuts its way into the hole, helping to secure it. In addition, some plastic filler was forced into the hole before the stanchion was pushed home.

The handrail was fitted into the bottom holes and the height of the rail adjusted and made parallel to the parapet. The subsequent stanchions were then fed on to the wire and pushed into the holes one by one. The handrail wire in this instance was not long

The completed viaduct set in its valley. The landscape has been created following the details in Tony Hill's **Creating Realistic Landscapes for Model Railways** *also published by Crowood.*

enough to run from one end of the parapet to the other, so needed to be joined. I had some small-bore brass tube that fitted the wire. A short length was cut to sleeve over each piece of wire at the joint. The stanchions were then secured with superglue. Once this had cured, the top rail was pulled through, again with a joint.

COLOURING STONE

Stonework colour varies according to the stone used in the structure. Sandstones are brown or even deep red, limestones grey or nearly white and granites grey.

The abutments of the plate-girder bridge have been made with heavily embossed plasticard that can be used to represent several types of stone

according to colour. I have chosen to make them grey/brown. The method can be used for other colours.

During assembly they were completed with a coating of filler used to fill the exposed open sections of the embossing on the corners and to add a fine texture to the surface. As it comes, the plasticard is shiny and smooth and that can be reflected in the finishing paint. Rather than acrylic primer, matt emulsion paint has been used as a base to colour.

PAINTING THE STONE

I have used artist's acrylic for painting the abutment. Its viscous properties, as comes from the tube, or its water solubility can be exploited on the heavy embossing. As before, when using these paints a palette is a necessity for mixing.

The stonework begins to change colour.

Charcoal grey (or it could be another grey) and white side by side on the palette. A wide, flat brush is collecting both paints but not mixing them, as can be seen by the discrete brush marks. The paint has not been diluted.

The abutment area to be painted is wetted with water – sufficient to make a shine, not swimming wet. The brush loaded with both colours is applied and drawn across the stonework. The colours mix as they are wetted.

The stonework is now an all-over mottled grey. The crevices in the surface tend to pick up particular colours, as there is a little more water held here than on the rest of the surface in the background, enhancing the effect. In addition, the brush loaded with mostly the darker grey has been drawn up the stonework, leaving paint on the underside of the stones. This creates areas of shadow.

LEFT: **Brown paint being applied over the top of the grey. The brush is being pulled down, leaving the colour on the upper side of the stones. The intensity can be varied by the amount of paint on the brush and the pressure applied to the bristles. The grey is still showing through the brown.**

BELOW: **A final wash of ochre has been added in places. This can be followed by a dark wash to represent staining running down from the bridge girders. This is best done with the girder in place.**

At this stage the abutment looks as if it is part of a black and white photograph, so needs some colour adding. Once dry, artist's acrylics are waterproof, so further colour can be added without affecting earlier ones.

FINISHING THE PLATE GIRDER

At the completion of construction, the plate girder was sprayed with acrylic matt black rather than grey. This serves the same purpose as painting the other structures grey. The black needs finishing and 'weathering'. As it stands it recedes, making a

black hole in the background. It requires lightening and other age effects added. The first step is to add rust. Generally this will be light on a well-maintained structure but occasionally it can develop into something more severe. The rust will tend to be near the bottom of the structure, as that is where the corrosive elements will settle: water and the sulphurous products of combustion in steam locomotives.

Light rust can be a staining on the surface; heavier rust will take on a three-dimensional effect as it flakes off the surface. Light rust is just an application of paint. Heavy rust can be achieved with a modifi-

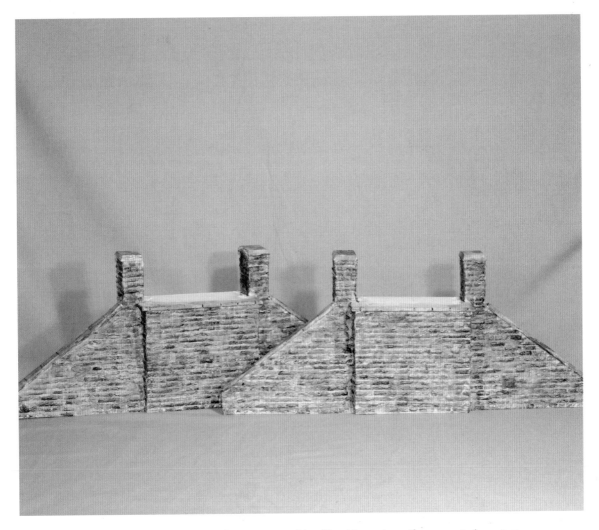

A pair of finished abutments. When working on something like this work on them as a pair, not as individuals, to achieve a consistent finish.

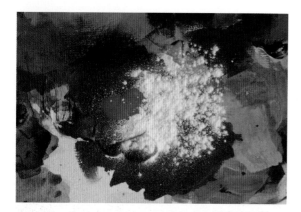 

The paint and talcum powder on the palette. Put the paint down first before adding the talc. I use basic unperfumed talc. There is no reason that perfumed talc cannot be used, I just don't like the perfumes that are added. The paint is stirred into the talc to make a paste. There is no change of colour. Do not use your best brushes for this – an old and frayed one is good enough, especially as the paint is stippled on.

The paint/talc mix has been applied in a corner where more extensive corrosion is likely to occur. Notice the 3D effect of the paint. In the photo the paint is still wet and will become matt as it dries. To illustrate this effect, I have added it after the other weathering effects have been added. It should go on before so that it picks up those effects.

Rust is added as a stain along edges and corners. The paint density varies depending where it is: densest in corners, thinnest where it is on a surface. This is a useful effect. The black remains very dense.

A pale grey wash is painted over everything. This removes the blackness. The bridge could be sprayed with a very dark grey instead of black for a similar effect but would lack the brush marks that here emphasize a rain-washed surface.

My weathering powder set. There are twelve colours, mostly earth and rust, but also green and blue. So far I have not found a use for the latter.

cation to the paint by adding talcum powder to give it body.

Now the finish has been toned down the final effects can be added. I use weathering powders for this; mine come from an American company called Bragdon Enterprises. They are very fine and have an

adhesive included in the powder, so no subsequent fixing is needed. The set I have is illustrated.

I have found that the best tool for applying the powders is a make-up brush. These can found at the appropriate counter in a number of stores. I mostly use one that is around 12mm ($\frac{1}{2}$in) wide. There are larger ones that can be used to spread the powder over larger areas. They are very soft and there is no danger of damaging any details.

After all the work that has gone into producing the rivet detail it needs to be noticed. This is best emphasized by 'dry brushing', where the paintbrush has very little paint in the bristles, most of it having been removed by brushing on to another surface. The brush is then lightly dragged across the detail and the high spots, like the bump of a rivet or an edge, will pick up such paint as is left on the brush. This just highlights the features.

Notwithstanding my descriptions here I would recommend an excellent book by Martyn Welch, *The Art of Weathering* published by Wild Swan (ISBN1 874103 11 9); this covers many techniques.

Further enhancing the rust paint with rust powder. The powder is collected on the brush and distributed to the areas where it is to be used. It is then worked into the surface with the brush. A little powder goes a long way.

The rivet detail on top of the girder dry brushed to highlight the rivets. On the right-hand end I have slightly too much paint on the brush, so it has left some brush marks on the surface next to the rivets. These were removed by dry brushing black rather than grey in the opposite direction. Further to the left the rivets and the end of the strap have collected the paint, as it should be just defining an edge and the rivets.

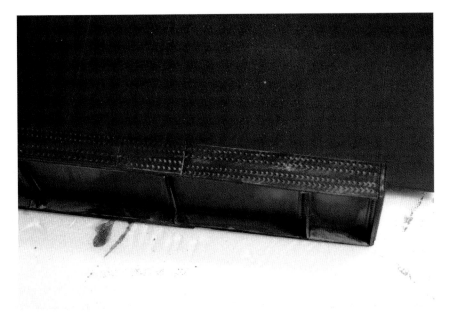

All done, a dirty bridge on its abutments. All that it needs now is a railway to go on it.

SUPPLIERS AND USEFUL ADDRESSES

*Note. Solvent adhesives and some paints cannot be sent via Royal Mail.

Slater's Plastikard Ltd
Old Road
Darley Dale
Matlock
Derbyshire
DE4 2ER
http://www.slatersplastikard.com/

Plain and embossed plasticard sheet; MEKPAK adhesive.*

Eileen's Emporium
Unit 19.1 Highnam Business Centre
Newent Road
Gloucester
GL2 8DN
http://www.eileensemporium.com/

Plain and embossed plasticard sheet; MEKPAK adhesive; Plastruct and Evergreen plastic sections; tools and metals.* Weathering powders.

C. and L. Finescale Modelling Ltd
Aran Lodge
Severn Road
Hallen
Bristol
BS10 7RZ
http://www.finescale.org.uk/

Butanone adhesive; Wills scenic products – 4mm bridges and retaining walls; Peco scenic products – 4 and 7mm; 4 and 7mm track components.*

Peco
Underleys
Beer
Devon
EX12 3NA
http://www.peco-uk.com/

2 and 4mm bridges and viaducts.

E. M. A. Model Supplies Ltd
14 Beadman Street
London
SE27 0DN
http://www.ema-models.co.uk/

Plain and embossed plasticard sheet; adhesives; Plastruct plastic sections; tools and metals.*

Many of these items can also be purchased through good local model shops, many of whom stock enamel and acrylic paints from Humbrol, Revell and Citadel. Humbrol are now producing a range of weathering powders. A range can also be found under the name of MIG.

Bragdon Enterprises
2960 Garden Tower Lane
Georgetown
CA 95634
USA
http://www.bragdonent.com/

Weathering powders.

Institution of Civil Engineers (ICE)
1 Great George Street
London
SW1P 3AA
http://www.ice.org.uk/

ICE has an archive of structures going back to the early days of railways. An enquiry to archive@ice.org.uk will find out if they have drawings of the structure you are interested in. ICE membership is not required.

Network Rail
Kings Place
90 York Way
London
N1 9AG
http://www.networkrail.co.uk/
http://www.networkrail.co.uk/VirtualArchive/

When I telephoned Network Rail to see if they could supply details of a structure they kept referring me to the National Railway Museum (NRM) at York.

See NRM details below. They do not seem to be set up to respond to telephone enquiries about civil engineering questions. A letter may elicit a better response. The archive link is developing but mainly features famous structures.

National Railway Museum (NRM)
Leeman Road
York YO26 4XJ
http://www.nrm.org.uk/

Their research facilities are excellent but for civil engineering drawings they have a limited collection of structures in the North East derived from the North Eastern Railway Company. Their photographic collection will be worth searching.

BOOKS AND MAGAZINES

The huge library of published railway books is a vast resource of pictures and sometime plans for bridges and viaducts. Many of the railway magazines have useful pictures too.

INDEX

RELATED TITLES FROM CROWOOD

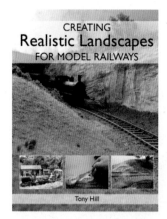

Creating Realistic Landscapes for Model Railways

TONY HILL

ISBN 978 1 84797 219 4

160pp, 400 illustrations

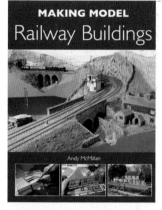

Making Model Railway Buildings

ANDY McMILLAN

ISBN 978 1 84797 340 5

288pp, 620 illustrations

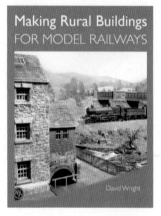

Making Rural Buildings for Model Railways

DAVID WRIGHT

ISBN 978 1 84797 460 0

192pp, 320 illustrations

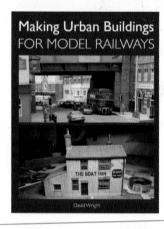

Making Urban Buildings for Model Railways

DAVID WRIGHT

ISBN 978 1 84797 568 3

192pp, 340 illustrations

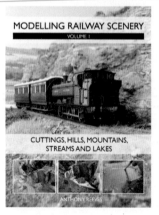

Modelling Railway Scenery

ANTHONY REEVES

ISBN 978 1 84797 619 2

160pp, 310 illustrations

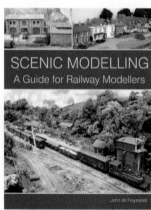

Scenic Modelling

JOHN DE FRAYSSINET

ISBN 978 1 84797 457 0

160pp, 230 illustrations

In case of difficulty ordering, please contact the Sales Office:

The Crowood Press, Ramsbury, Wiltshire SN8 2HR UK

Tel: 44 (0) 172 520320   enquiries@crowood.com   www.crowood.com